Accessible
HOME

Updating Your Home for Changing Physical Needs

CREATIVE
PUBLISHING
international

CHANHASSEN, MINNESOTA
www.creativepub.com

© Copyright 2003
Creative Publishing international, Inc.
18705 Lake Drive East
Chanhassen, Minnesota 55317
1-800-328-3895
www.creativepub.com
All rights reserved

Printed by Quebecor World
10 9 8 7 6 5 4 3 2 1

President/CEO: Michael Eleftheriou
Vice President/Publisher: Linda Ball
Vice President/Retail Sales & Marketing: Kevin Haas

Executive Editor: Bryan Trandem
Creative Director: Tim Himsel
Managing Editor: Michelle Skudlarek
Editorial Director: Jerri Farris

Author & Lead Editor: Nancy Baldrica
Senior Art Director: David Schelitzche
Editors: Karen Ruth, Phil Schmidt, Brett Martin
Copy Editor: Karen Ruth
Project Manager: Andrew Karre
Mac Designers: Jon Simpson, Andrew Karre
Technical Photo Editors: Paul Gorton, Dane Smith
Illustrator: Jon Simpson
Photo Researchers: Julie Caruso, Andrew Karre, Katherine Schmidt
Studio Services Manager: Jeanette Moss McCurdy
Photo Team Leader: Tate Carlson
Photographer: Tate Carlson
Scene Shop Carpenters: Randy Austin
Director of Production Services and Photography: Kim Gerber
CREATING THE ACCESSIBLE HOME
Created by: The Editors of Creative Publishing international, Inc.

Other titles from Creative Publishing international include:
New Everyday Home Repairs, Decorating With Paint & Wallcovering, Basic Wiring & Electrical Repairs, Advanced Home Wiring, Landscape Design & Construction, Bathroom Remodeling, Built-In Projects for the Home, Refinishing & Finishing Wood, Home Masonry Repairs & Projects, Building Porches & Patios, Flooring Projects & Techniques, Advanced Home Plumbing, Remodeling Kitchens, Carpentry: Remodeling, Carpentry: Tools•Shelves•Walls•Doors, Great Decks, Building Decks, Advanced Deck Building, Stonework & Masonry Projects, Finishing Basements & Attics, Sheds, Gazebos & Outbuildings, Customizing Your Home, Building & Finishing Walls & Ceilings, The Complete Guide to Home Plumbing, The Complete Guide to Home Wiring, The Complete Guide to Building Decks, The Complete Guide to Painting & Decorating, The Complete Guide to Creative Landscapes, The Complete Guide to Home Masonry, The Complete Guide to Home Carpentry, The Complete Guide to Home Storage, The Complete Guide to Windows & Doors, The Complete Guide to Bathrooms, The Complete Photo Guide to Home Repair, The Complete Photo Guide to Home Improvement, The Complete Photo Guide to Outdoor Home Improvement.

Cover and backcover photos courtesy of Elkay, GE, Kohler Co., Weiser Lock, The Swan Corporation, and L.E. Johnson Products.

Library of Congress Cataloging-in-Publication Data

Creating the accessible home: updating your home for changing physical needs.
     p. cm.
    Includes index.
    ISBN 1-58923-061-2 (soft cover)
    1. Dwellings--Remoldeling. 2. Dwellings--Access for the physi-
cally handicapped. 3. Barrier-free design. I. Creative Publishing
International.
TH4816.15. C74 2002
643'.7--dc21   2002035047

CONTENTS

©Robert Perron

3

INTRODUCTION

I f you're reading this book, there's a good chance that you, or someone close to you, faces physical challenges as a result of genetic disorder, disease, accident, or aging.

During the writing of this book, I learned first-hand the frustration and anger a person feels with a sudden loss of independence. When my mother had a stroke, she literally lost her independence overnight. The active, independent woman I had always known suddenly needed help taking a shower and getting her coffee.

I came to realize that it was important to find a balance between safety and independence for both my mother and me. The ideas in this book suddenly made sense to me. Putting an elevated seat on the toilet meant my mother could care for herself in the bathroom. Clearing walkways allowed her to move with a walker without tripping and falling. Moving dishes and coffee cups to a lower cabinet helped her prepare her own meals.

These small changes made a big difference. They not only let my mother maintain some independence, they gave me—and the rest of the family—peace of mind. We knew that my mother was safer and happier.

My experience is just one example of how the ideas presented in this book can be used. There are many others.

Photo courtesy of Wellborn Cabinets.

TOM

Tom's son, Mark, was born with muscular dystrophy.

When Mark was small, the family cared for him as they would any young child. They fed him, clothed him, and bathed him.

But as Mark grew older, he wanted to do more for himself. He didn't want his mother to pick out his clothes or his father to help him take a shower. He wanted to be more independent.

That's when the family realized they had to make some changes. They had cleared walkways long ago for Mark's wheelchair. When Mark turned 10, the family decided to add an elevator to the house so Mark could get to his bedroom on his own. They also redesigned the upstairs bath to include a roll-in shower with a hand-held sprayer, which allowed Mark to bathe himself. And they added an adjustable closet system in the bedroom that Mark shares with his older brother.

"We really weighed our options," Tom said. "We thought about moving, but we didn't want to uproot our other children. By changing our existing home, we helped Mark be just another member of the household.

"It was good because the changes didn't disrupt the rest of the family. My other children can use the upstairs bathroom just as easily as Mark. And the adjustable closet system lets Mark pick out his own clothes, but it keeps his brother's stuff handy, too.

"Putting in the elevator ended up being one of the best changes we made. It's great for Mark, but it's a big help to his mom and me, too. We used to carry Mark up and down the stairs, but he was getting heavy. And let's face it—we're not getting any younger, either. My wife's knees are getting arthritic, so now we use the elevator to carry laundry and other stuff upstairs. It's been great!"

Even outdoor patio and garden spaces can be wheelchair accessible with some creative landscaping ideas.

MARY

Mary's husband, John, was in a car accident that broke his back and left him unable to reach or bend.

During his recovery, he relied on Mary to help him reach things. After John's back healed, Mary decided to make some permanent changes in the house.

"The doctors told us that John was going to have trouble bending and reaching for the rest of his life, and I realized I couldn't always be there to help him," Mary said.

"We took a look around the house and discovered there were a lot of things that were going to be difficult for John. He couldn't even reach the window blinds if the sun was shining in!

"We talked to his occupational therapist and asked for some recommendations. She helped us evaluate each room and gave us some great suggestions.

"We ended up adding remote-controlled window blinds in the bedroom, which was a simple change. And we added some pull-out drawers and pop-up shelves so John can help out in the kitchen.

"But I think the change that John appreciated the most was reorganizing his workshop, so he could reach his tools easier. He loves to tinker, and now he still can. We just added some pegboard and hooks to the side of his workbench, so he didn't have to reach for his equipment. And we had the electrician install some raised outlets so John could plug in his power tools without bending to the floor.

"The changes that I really enjoy are the raised flower beds and garden spigot outside. John can reach the planters and the hose, but I like that the flowers are at eye level. It's really nice.

"Before the accident, I didn't realize how inconvenient so many things were in the house. I just put up with reaching into the back of my cabinets and lifting heavy mixers onto the counter. Things are a lot easier for me now, too."

Small changes help family members maintain independence and offer peace of mind to their caregivers.

THIS BOOK

This book will help you make every area of the home more accessible, from living and entertaining areas to kitchens, baths, office and hobby rooms, garage and storage areas, and outdoor living spaces.

Each chapter takes a look at one area of your home, giving you simple suggestions and easy projects to make your home more accessible. You'll also find information specific to wheelchair and walker users.

The ideas presented in this book are based on the concept of universal design, a theory developed from a belief that houses should serve the people who live in them.

Universal design acknowledges that people come in all shapes and sizes, with varying abilities. The concept combines the areas of occupational and physical therapy, architecture, human physiology, and home building

to present straightforward ideas for good home design. You are sure to find many ideas to use in your home. And you'll be pleased to discover that the solutions benefit every member of your family.

The best part of universal design is its timeless appeal. These ideas won't go out of style. In fact, the projects presented in this book are likely to increase the value of your home and make it more marketable to a broader base of homebuyers.

The last part of this book provides sources for home-modification funding, advice on how to find and hire contractors, and resources for support and information on disabilities and accessibility. The listings often provide federal sources, but you'll find many state and local agencies offer support in your area. Check your Yellow Pages for organizations close to home.

Before you make any modifications to your home, consult your doctor, physical therapist, or occupational therapist to discuss your plans. These professionals are familiar with your particular case and can give you helpful advice for your situation.

Accessible homes serve both the disabled and able-bodied people who live in them (above).

Many accessibility modifications blend into a home's decor, like a kitchen faucet with a lever handle and pull-out sprayer (left).

©Robert Perron

Depending on the extent of your plans for modification, you may also want to contact a home designer or builder who specializes in universal design or accessible housing to discuss ideas and draw up plans.

As always, before you begin a home-improvement project, consult your local building department regarding codes and regulations. Professionals in the department can tell you what work you can complete yourself and what must be hired out to a contractor.

Above all, remember that the ideas offered here are a starting point. The goal is to make your home safer and more accessible for every person in your home. Tailor your modifications to your family.

ACCESSIBILITY CONSIDERATIONS

Vision: Reduce glare, mark room and counter-top boundaries, clear walking paths, improve lighting.

Hearing: Hang window and wall coverings, incorporate visual alerts.

Mobility: Reorganize cabinets, use specialty shelving, automate windows and shades, install intercoms and remote locks.

Strength: Replace knobs with lever handles, change cabinet pulls to C handles or magnetic latches, install rocker switches.

Wheelchairs/Walkers: Clear pathways, widen doorways, check thresholds, replace thick pile or slippery flooring, create roll-under spaces.

Talk to your doctor, physical therapist, or occupational therapist about modifications that will benefit you and your family.

LIVING & ENTERTAINING AREAS

Living and entertaining areas represent your home's personality, providing the backdrop for relaxing with family and friends. You want everyone who enters these rooms to be greeted with comfort, beauty, accessibility, and safety.

Some simple changes in design and purpose can often make the biggest differences in these rooms. For example, installing specialty switches can make nighttime visits to the kitchen or bathroom safer, and adding track lighting can brighten work areas and help prevent accidents. If you're ready for a bigger home improvement project, you'll find step-by-step instructions for widening a doorway or installing a pocket door for better wheelchair or walker access.

No matter what changes you choose, you'll be pleased to find the ideas presented here will envelop family and friends in beauty, while providing accessiblity.

©Robert Perron

Floor Plan

People with mobility and vision problems require clear walking paths so they can navigate a room easily. Create clear floor space by moving furniture and accessories out of walking areas. Allow enough space to reach furniture without bumping into coffee tables or decorations. Maintain intimacy in large, open rooms by dividing them into smaller, "special use" spaces.

■ **Wheelchair & Walker Modifications:**

• Move furniture against walls to create clear space for moving and turning.

Flooring

Make sure all flooring in living and entertaining areas is nonslip and level. For people with vision or mobility problems, remove or secure area rugs with carpet tape to prevent tripping.

If you're replacing flooring, choose matte finishes in wood, glazed ceramic tile, level stone, vinyl, or cork to reduce glare. In carpeting, look for low pile, low-level loop, or industrial styles that provide surer footing and prevent tripping. Consider a complementary color or pattern along the room's edge to help people with vision problems mark boundaries.

Take special care to check transition areas where rooms meet and flooring height varies. Square thresholds should be offset by no more than ¼", and slanted thresholds by no more than ½". If transitions are higher than ½", remove or replace thresholds, or install transition wedges.

■ **Wheelchair & Walker Modifications:**

• Make sure transitions between rooms have vertical offsets that are no higher than ¼", or install transition wedges.

• Choose nonslip, matte finishes in wood, glazed ceramic tile, level stone, vinyl, or cork. In carpeting, select low pile, low-level loop, or industrial styles.

Lighting/Electrical

Increase light at the front door's keyhole and keypad so people with vision and mobility problems can unlock the door quickly. Sufficient lighting will also aid residents in clearly identifying guests before they are allowed to enter the home. For convenience, fit all entryway light fixtures with long-life, full-spectrum lightbulbs that do not need to be replaced as often.

Entryway thresholds (above) can be made more accessible with a variety of easily installed products.

Divide family rooms (left) into mutiple-use areas that can be altered for adaptability. The roll-under desk provides easy access for wheelchairs when the desk chair is moved. The beanbag is easily moved to provide clear floor space.

Touch lights are handy home accessories that can be added to closets, stairways, and entries. Since they don't require wiring, they're quick and easy to install.

Inside the house, convert lamp knobs or pull-chains to touch switches. These handy plug-in devices are particularly helpful to people with limited hand strength or coordination.

Change toggle switches on wall and ceiling fixtures to rocker switches that offer easy manipulation. Consider lighted styles so people with limited vision can locate them quickly.

If limited mobility or memory is an issue, automate lighting with occcupancy sensor lights that turn on and off when someone enters or leaves a room. Or consider programmable lighting and heating systems, which are preset to run throughout the day and night. (See page 33 for switch installation.)

When replacing switches, install 3- or 4-way switches so lights can be activated from several locations, and add switches near bathrooms and bedrooms for nighttime safety.

In family areas, install track lights to eliminate shadows and glare and to highlight different activity areas. (See page 34 for track lighting installation.)

(See page 33 for switch installation.)

(See page 34 for track lighting installation.)

TIP: LIGHTBULBS

Cast a whole new light in your home with specialized lightbulbs. Newer varieties include halogens, full-spectrum bulbs, colored glass, and exciting shapes. Many provide illumination that simulates sunlight, which enhances vision for people with limited sight.

Occupancy sensor lights turn lights on and off automatically when someone enters or leaves the room. They make nighttime travel through the house safer.

■ Wheelchair & Walker Modifications:

• Wall-mount track lighting, so lights can be adjusted and bulbs can be replaced easily.

• Raise electrical outlet heights to between 18 and 30" above floor level.

Stairways

Keep stairways free of clutter, especially for people with limited vision or mobility, by using stairway baskets to hold and transfer items to other levels of the house. If stairways are dark, install additional lighting fixtures. Or use touch lights, which do not require wiring, to illuminate them.

Also consider closing off open-riser stairs, whose depth can be difficult to gauge and negotiate. If the steps themselves are too shallow, use tread extensions to deepen them. Most building codes now require steps to be at least 10" deep.

Make sure every stairway of two or more steps has a railing, and consider extending rails past the top and bottom stairs for added stability. (See page 19 for handrail installation.)

Set handrails at a comfortable height, and consider two handrails—one set between 34 and 38" and another set at 24"—for people of various heights.

Photo courtesy of Basketville.

Stairway baskets reduce clutter on stairs and make carrying small items up and down stairs easier.

It's also a good idea to mount handrails on both sides of stairwells and in the middle of wide stairways so family members can use either arm for support. This is an important consideration for someone who has suffered a stroke.

Make sure railings remain safe by checking them regularly and tightening them often. A railing must be capable of supporting 250 pounds.

If stairs are particularly difficult for a family member, consider installing a stairlift. Styles are available to accommodate corners and curves, as well as straight runs. Look for a seat and motor capacity that fits your home and family comfortably.

■ Wheelchair & Walker Modifications:

• Add an elevator for access to every floor of your home. Some models can be installed in converted, stacked closet space, and others are free-standing.

Photo courtesy of Bruno Independent Living.

Add a stairlift when navigating stairs is particularly difficult for a family member. Stairlifts come in a variety of styles to accommodate both straight and curved stairways.

Doorways

Provide level, protected entryways so people with vision or mobility problems can escape the elements and enter the house safely and comfortably. A package shelf near the doorway frees hands to unlock and open doors.

Make sure door hardware is easy to use by replacing doorknobs with lever handles that open with a push, or install a keyless entry system (page 106) that operates by touch.

An automatic door opener is another good option. These devices attach to existing doors to automatically open, close, and lock entrances by remote control or touch pad. Look for styles that offer customized hold-open settings for safe passage through the doorway.

To improve security for the elderly, people with vision problems, and those who live alone, add sidelights or peepholes to doors so guests can be identified before they enter the house. Hang sheer curtains on side panels to provide privacy and reduce glare.

For added convenience, install an intercom system that allows family members to see and/or hear guests at the door. Some models offer remote control so doors can be opened from anywhere in the house—a helpful feature for people with limited mobility or hand strength.

■ **Wheelchair & Walker Modifications:**

• Replace regular hinges with swing-clear hinges that provide wider passageways.

• Widen doorways to 32 to 36", with 36" preferred. (See page 21 for door-widening instructions.)

• Add a ramp (page 124) to a side, back, or front entrance, or install an electric lift outdoors or in an attached garage.

Windows

Reduce glare from large sunny windows by installing window films or by hanging full-length draperies in homes of people with vision problems. Automated, remote-controlled window coverings allow for easy adjustment of light levels and privacy.

If a family member has hearing difficulties,

TIP: LEVER HANDLES

Lever handles are easier to use than traditional doorknobs. They are especially beneficial to people with limited hand strength, because they can be activated by any part of the body. As a general rule, install door hardware at a maximum height of 44 to 48".

Weiser Lock.®/Rick Gayle Studios.

Photo courtesy of Simpson Door Co.

Exterior lighting provides home security, welcomes family and guests, and helps prevent falls.

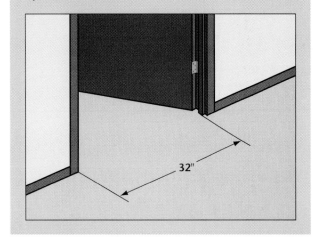
select heavy window fabrics for draperies and shades to absorb interior sound and enhance conversation.

Casement windows with sill-level latches are easiest to operate for people with reduced hand strength or mobility.

■ **Wheelchair & Walker Modifications:**

• Install remote-control window covering systems.

• Reposition windows so wheelchair users can see outside.

• When replacing windows, choose casement windows with lock latches at sill height.

Photo left courtesy of Smarthome, Inc.

Remote-controlled window coverings are an affordable option that offers safety and convenience.

Wall Coverings

Cover walls with small, simple wallpaper patterns or matte-finish paint in neutral colors for people with limited vision. Bright, busy, wallpaper can be distracting and glossy walls produce glare.

If limited hearing is an issue, opt for wallpaper to help absorb sound, limit background noise, and enhance conversation.

Furniture

If you have large, overstuffed furniture, consider replacing it with firm, upright pieces that are more comfortable for people with back problems or limited arm or leg strength. Avoid rocking chairs and other unstable furniture that might give way if used for balance.

Select soft upholstery fabrics rather than leather, which can inhibit movement, and choose furniture that fits comfortably. Knees should bend at the seat's edge, the lower back and neck should be supported, and elbows should form a right angle to armrests.

Intercom doorbells help family members identify guests at the door.

Photo courtesy of Smarthome, Inc.

Casement windows are easy to operate, and they provide excellent safety exits for bedrooms and basements. Look for models that feature single-lever locking systems–like the one shown here–that are located close to the sill. For added convenience, consider adding an automatic window opener.

Photos used with permission of Anderson Corporation.

Choose simple patterns with matte finishes for walls, draperies, and upholstery (left) for people with vision problems. Busy patterns on walls and fabrics can be distracting (right).

HANDRAILS

Adding handrails to long hallways or living areas can offer elderly and disabled people the extra support they need to move safely through the home.

Purchase prefabricated handrails and other stair-related parts through your local lumberyard's millwork desk or order them directly from a stair part manufacturer.

Building codes typically call for a handrail diameter of 1¼ to 2⅜", so choose a size that's easy to grab between your thumb and fingers. Smooth, round handrails usually offer the best grip.

Select mounting hardware that can support a minimum of 250 pounds at any point along the rail, and anchor brackets properly to wall studs. If you must install a bracket where there is no stud, use a toggle bolt or other anchor rated to 250 pounds.

Finally, position your handrail 1½" from the wall to leave room to grip the bar and prevent a gap large enough to capture an arm. (See the tip box below for suggested handrail heights.)

TIP: STAIRWAY HANDRAILS

Building codes around the country require handrails to be mounted 34 to 38" high on at least one side of every stairway with two or more steps. But you may have to go beyond that requirement to ensure safety for your family. Wheelchair users, for example, benefit from handrails mounted between 27 and 29" on ramps. Children need lower handrails—around 24"—for safety. And elderly family members benefit from railings installed on both sides of every stairway, as well as down the middle of wide stairways.

Handrail ends must terminate into the wall or have a turnout or easing at the bottom of the stairs (inset). At a minimum, handrails must extend from a point directly above the bottom riser to a point directly above the top riser.

For increased support, extend the railing with two horizontal sections at both ends: 12" beyond the top riser, and 12" plus the depth of one tread beyond the bottom riser. This is especially important for an elderly person or someone with vision problems.

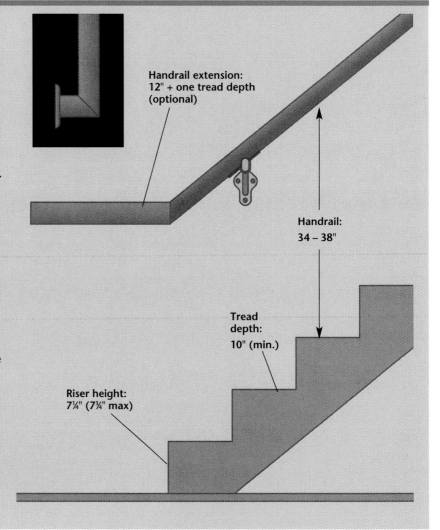

Handrail extension: 12" + one tread depth (optional)

Handrail: 34 – 38"

Tread depth: 10" (min.)

Riser height: 7¼" (7¾" max)

HOW TO INSTALL A HORIZONTAL HANDRAIL ALONG A WALL

STEP A: *Mark the Handrail Height*

1. Subtract the height of the support bracket from the desired height of the handrail.

2. At each end of the project wall, measure up from the floor and mark the wall at the height of the bottom of the support bracket. Snap a chalk line through the marks.

STEP B: *Install the Support Brackets*

1. Use a studfinder to locate the wall studs, and mark the stud centers with light pencil marks just below the chalk line.

2. Center each support bracket over a stud marking so its bottom edge is on the chalk line. Use a small level to make sure the bracket is plumb, then mark the screw holes onto the wall.

3. Drill pilot holes for the screws through the drywall and into the studs. Install the support brackets with screws.

STEP C: *Attach the Railing*

1. Position the railing on the brackets so it rests 1½" from the wall. Clamp the railing in place.

2. Secure the railing to the top ends of the brackets using screws driven through pilot holes.

3. Test the railing by applying weight at various points. Tighten any loose screws.

A. *Mark the height of your handrail, and snap a chalk line along the wall.*

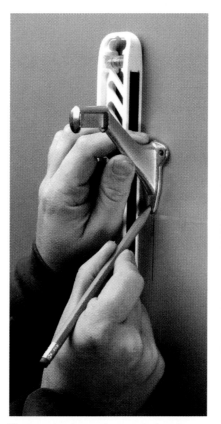

B. *Use a level to make sure the brackets are plumb. Then mark and drill pilot holes, and fasten the brackets to the wall.*

C. *Set the railing and clamp it in place, then screw it to the support brackets.*

WIDER DOORWAYS

Standard doorways can limit movement for people who use walkers and wheelchairs. Doorway openings of 32 to 36" offer better access.

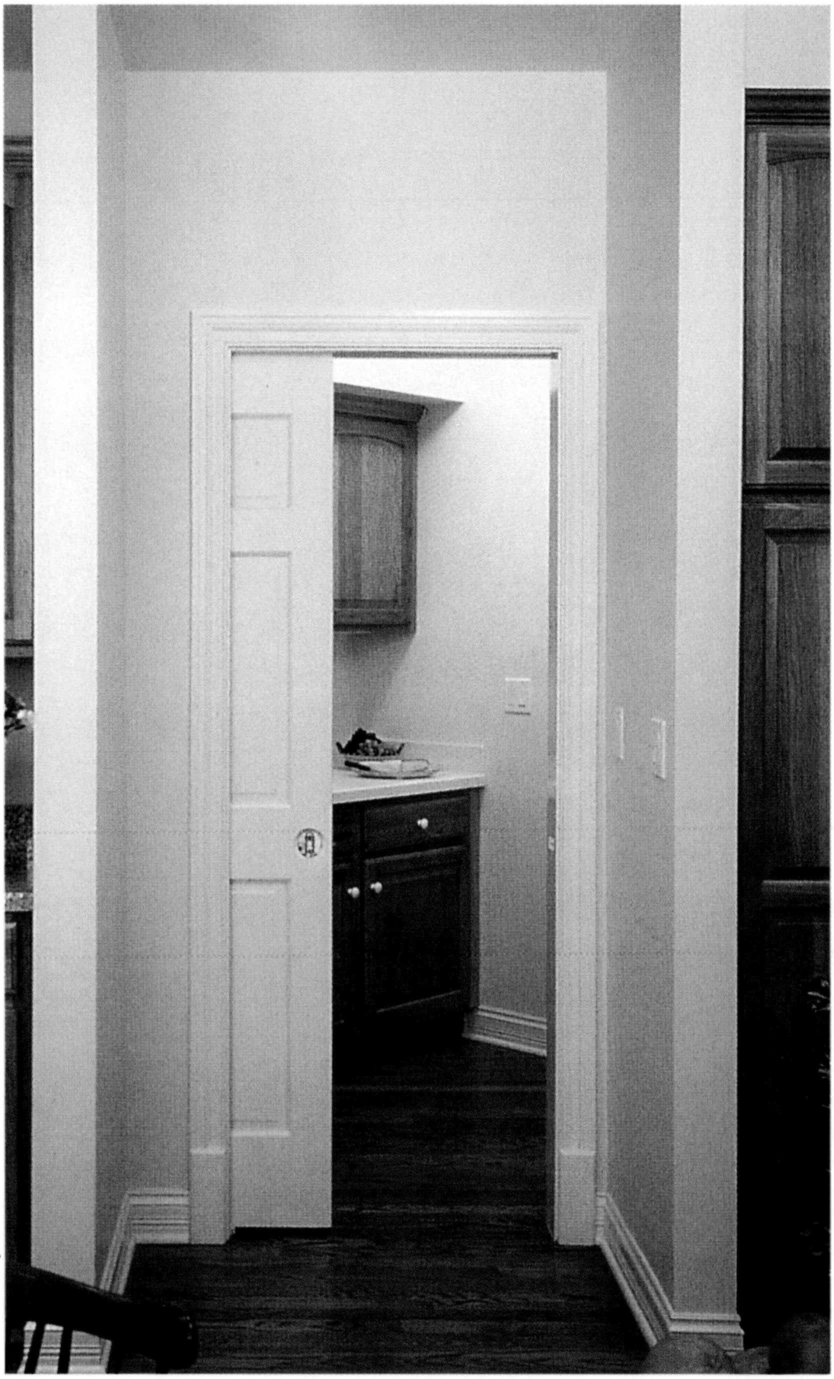

There are several ways to increase doorway width. You can remove the door and hinges to gain an additional 1½ to 2" of space. Removing the door stops, the wood strips on the door frame, will add ¾ to 1" inch of extra clearance. Or you can replace standard hinges with swing-clear hinges, which open out and away from the doorway, to gain space equal to the door's thickness.

Before you replace hinges, evaluate the door's swing. Some room designs do not permit the extra space required by swing-clear hinges. Where door swing is an issue, consider installing a sliding door. Some models can be installed on the outside of door frames, rather than in the wall.

If you need more room than these simple fixes provide, you can widen the door opening and install a prehung replacement door. Measure carefully to ensure that there is room for the wider door to swing open. If space does not permit a wider swinging door, consider installing the pocket door shown on pages 26 to 29. Although both of these projects are time consuming with many steps, none of the steps requires more than basic carpentry skills.

The project shown here begins with removing the existing door and surrounding wall surfaces, reframing the door opening, installing a prehung interior door, and refinishing the wall surfaces. The directions given are for a non-loadbearing wall. You must make sure your wall is non-loadbearing before you start this project because loadbearing walls require special bracing and larger header sizes. If you need to replace a door in an interior loadbearing wall or an exterior wall, consult a professional.

Before you cut into the wall, examine the area around the door to locate mechanicals inside the walls. Look directly above and below the project area to see what plumbing, wiring, or ductwork might extend vertically between floors. Don't forget to look at both sides of the walls—there might be an outlet or switch on one side, but not the other. Original blueprints of your house also can help you locate utility lines. If necessary, have the utility lines moved by a professional.

Because you will be widening the doorway by removing a section of wall, you will need to match the newly exposed floor to the existing floor surface or put in a replacement threshold. The difference in vertical height between the floor and threshold must be less than ¼" to allow for wheelchair access and to prevent tripping.

TOOLS & MATERIALS

- Hammer
- Screwdriver
- Pry bar
- Reciprocating saw
- Measuring tape
- Studfinder
- Plumb bob
- Circular saw
- Utility knife
- Drill
- Drywall T-square

- 4-ft. level
- Power miter saw
- Nail set
- 2 × 4 lumber
- 8d, 10d & 16d nails
- Drywall panels
- 1¼" coarse-thread drywall screws
- All-purpose drywall compound

- Paper joint tape
- 6" & 12" drywall knives
- 150-grit sanding sponge
- Prehung door unit
- Tapered wood shims
- Door casing
- 4d & 6d finish nails

HOW TO WIDEN AN INTERIOR DOORWAY IN A NON-LOADBEARING WALL
STEP A: *Prepare the Rough Opening*
1. Remove the old door by driving out the hinge pins with a hammer and screwdriver.
2. Use a pry bar and hammer to remove the door casing. If you intend to reuse the casing, pull the nails through the back sides of the pieces.

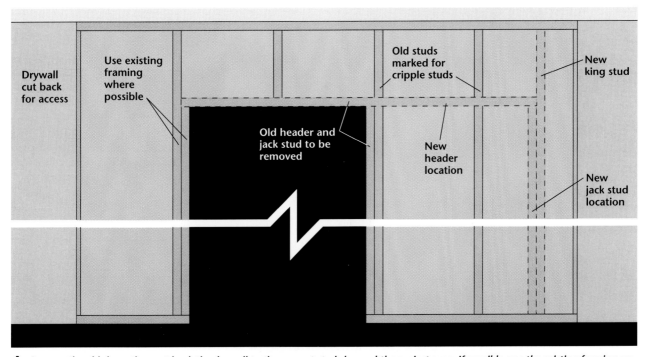

A. *Remove the old door, then cut back the drywall to the nearest studs beyond the project area. If possible, use the existing framing on one side of the door opening.*

3. Pull the nails securing the door jambs to the framing, or cut through the nails with a reciprocating saw. Remove the jambs from the opening.

4. Determine the width of the new rough opening by measuring the width of the new prehung door unit—at the outsides of the jambs—and adding 1" to the dimension. This will provide a ½" shim space on both sides of the new door unit.

5. Use a studfinder to locate the first stud to either side of the planned new rough opening. Mark a cutting line on the centers of the studs, and cut through the drywall with a utility knife or circular saw. If you use a circular saw, set the depth to match the thickness of the drywall. Use a hammer and pry bar to remove the drywall to the ceiling and floor between the cuts.

6. Carefully remove trim moldings or baseboards.

7. Mark the header for removal. Then use a reciprocating saw and hammer to remove the old header, jack stud, and king stud from the rough opening.

STEP B: *Install the New King Stud & Header*

1. Mark the width of the new rough opening using the dimension you calculated in step A. Measure from the inside face of the existing jack stud and mark the bottom wall plate. This mark represents the inside face of the new jack stud.

2. Measure over 1½" (away from the opening) and make another mark on the bottom plate. This mark represents the inside face of the new king stud.

3. Use a plumb bob or a level and a straight board to transfer the king and jack stud marks to the top wall plate.

4. Cut the king stud from a straight 2 × 4. It should fit snugly between the top and bottom plates.

5. Position the king stud on the marks and toenail it to the plates with three 8d nails at each end, driving the nails at an angle through the stud and into the plates.

6. Check the height of the rough opening by measuring from the floor to the top end of the existing jack stud. The height should be between ¼" and ¾" greater than the height of the new door unit. If the height falls within this range, you can use the existing jack stud. Mark the height of the existing jack stud onto the inside face of the new king stud. If the jack stud does not fall within the range, remove the jack stud, then mark the old and new

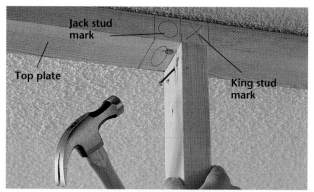

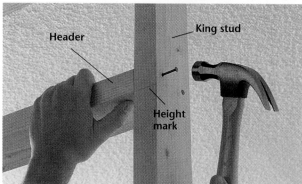

B. *Toenail the king stud to the plates (top), then mark the rough opening height. Install the header at the height mark (bottom).*

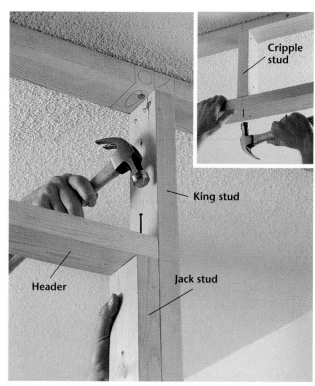

C. *Nail the header to the jack stud, then fasten the jack stud to the king stud. Install a cripple stud centered over the opening (inset).*

king studs at a height equal to the door unit height plus ½".

7. Cut a 2 × 4 header to fit between the king studs. Position the header so its bottom face is flush with the rough opening height marks (jack stud marks) and fasten it to the king stud with 16d nails.

STEP C: *Install the Jack & Cripple Studs*

1. Cut a new 2 × 4 jack stud to fit snugly under the header. Fasten the stud by nailing down through the header, then drive 10d nails through the face of the jack stud and into the king stud at 12" intervals.

2. Mark the center of the rough opening onto the side edge of the header. Cut a 2 × 4 cripple stud to fit snugly between the header and top plate.

3. Center the cripple stud over the mark and fasten it by nailing up through the header, then toenail it to the top plate.

4. Use a handsaw or reciprocating saw to cut off the end of the bottom plate so it is flush with the inside face of the new jack stud.

STEP D: *Hang the Drywall*

1. Plan the installation of the new drywall. If possible, use only one panel on each side, leaving only two seams to finish. If you need more than one panel, make sure the seam between the two new pieces falls on the center of the new cripple stud. Use panels of the same thickness as the existing drywall.

2. Cut each drywall panel to fit, using a utility knife and a T-square or straightedge. Make the overall length ½" shorter than the floor-to-ceiling dimension.

3. Position the panels with their top edges butted against the ceiling drywall and fasten them to the wall studs and plates with 1¼" coarse-thread drywall screws driven at 8" intervals. Drive the screws deep enough to dimple the surface without ripping the face paper.

STEP E: *Tape the Drywall*

1. Apply an even bed layer of all-purpose drywall compound over each seam, about ⅛" thick, using a 6" taping knife.

2. Lay a continuous strip of paper joint tape over the seam's center, and lightly embed it into the compound, making sure it's smooth and straight.

3. Smooth the tape with the taping knife, working outward from the center. Apply enough pressure to force compound from underneath the tape, leaving the tape flat and with a thin layer of compound underneath.

D. *Fasten the drywall panels to the framing every 8". Recess the screws slightly without tearing through the face paper (inset).*

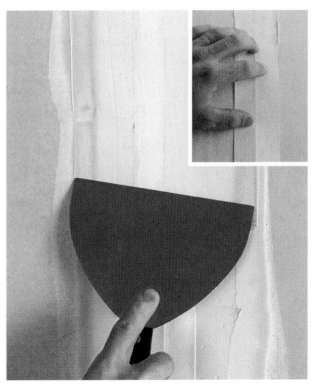

E. *Apply a thin layer of compound over each seam, then embed the tape (inset). Smooth the tape and compound with the taping knife.*

4. Cover all exposed screw heads with the first of three coats of compound (you don't need to cover those that will be behind the casing). Let the compound dry overnight.

STEP F: *Finish the Drywall*

1. Second-coat the taped seams with a thin, even layer of compound, using a 12" drywall knife. Smooth the sides of the compound first, holding the blade almost flat and applying pressure to the outside of the blade so that the blade just skims over the center of the seam.

2. After feathering both sides, make a pass down the center of the seam, leaving the seam smooth and even, the edges feathered out to nothing. Completely cover the joint tape and let dry overnight.

3. Apply another layer of compound over the screws, then let the entire second coat dry overnight.

4. Lightly sand the seams with a 150-grit sanding sponge. Apply a third coat of compound to the seams, using the same technique as with the second coat. Make sure the surface is smooth and flat.

5. Third-coat the screws, then let the compound dry completely.

6. Sand the compound lightly with the sanding sponge.

STEP G: *Set the New Door & Secure the Hinge Jamb*

1. Remove all of the fasteners or the strapping used to keep the door closed during shipping. Set the door into the framed opening so the jamb edges are flush with the drywall and the unit is centered from side to side in the opening. Using a level, adjust the unit so that the hinge jamb is plumb.

2. Starting near the top hinge, insert pairs of tapered wood shims (with the tapered ends opposed to form a flat surface) into the gap between the framing and the jamb, spaced every 12 inches. Slide the shims in until they are snug but not bending the jamb. Use the level to make sure the jamb is still plumb. Install shim pairs near each hinge.

3. Working down from the top, anchor the hinge jamb by driving 8d casing nails through the jamb and shims, into the framing members. Drive nails only at shim locations. Check the jamb with the level as you work to make sure it remains plumb and straight. Nail at the remaining shim locations.

STEP H: *Complete the Door Installation*

1. Insert pairs of shims into the gap between the

F. *Using a 12" drywall knife, apply a layer of compound to the seams. Smooth the sides of the seam first, then smooth the center.*

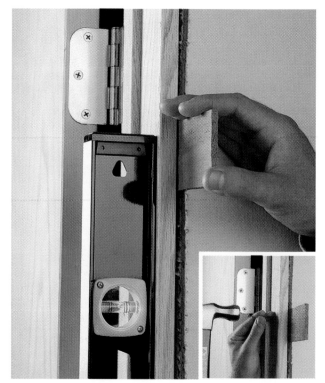

G. *Insert shim pairs at each hinge location, using a level to check for plumb. Secure the jamb and shims with casing nails (inset).*

framing and the latch jamb, aligning them roughly with the shims on the hinge jamb.

2. With the door closed, adjust the shims so the gap between the door and the jamb is consistent—usually ⅛"—from top to bottom. Nail at each shim location.

3. Install two pairs of shims between the top jamb and the framing, making sure they don't bow the jamb, and nail them in place.

4. Set all nails below the surface of the wood with a nail set. Using a handsaw or utility knife, carefully cut off the shims so they are flush with the wall surface.

STEP I: *Install the Casing*

1. Finish the new drywall to match the existing surface.

2. On the edge of each jamb, make short pencil marks about ⅛" from the inside edge—these setback marks represent the inside edges of the casing. Mark at both ends of each jamb, and make sure the amount of setback remains consistent.

3. Place a length of casing along one side jamb so the bottom end is on the floor and the inside edge is aligned with the setback marks. At the top corner of the door frame, mark the point where the vertical and horizontal setback lines meet.

4. Cut the casing with a 45° miter cut, using a power miter saw. Tack the piece into place with two 4d finish nails driven through the casing and into the jamb. Drill pilot holes for the nails to prevent splitting. At this stage, do not drive the nails flush.

5. Mark, cut, and tack up the casing on the other side of the door.

6. Cut the top casing piece to fit between the vertical pieces. Make sure the joints fit well, then drill pilot holes and attach the casing to the jambs with 4d finish nails driven about every 16". Drive 6d finish nails through the casing near the outer edge, into the wall framing. Drive all nail heads below the surface, using a nail set.

7. Reinstall the floor trim or baseboards.

8. Fill the nail holes with matching wood putty.

H. *Install shims along the latch jamb, making sure the gap between the door and jamb is consistent.*

I. *Make setback marks to help measure and position the casing. Nail the casing to the jambs and framing with finish nails.*

POCKET DOOR

Pocket doors require no threshold and are easy to open and close, making them a good alternative for wheelchair or walker users.

Be aware, however, that standard recessed latch hardware can be difficult to use, especially when hand strength is limited. Instead, opt for C handles, like those used in this project.

Pocket door hardware kits generally are universal and can be adapted for almost any interior door. In this project, the frame kit includes an adjustable track, steel-clad split studs, and all the required hanging hardware. The latch hardware, jambs, and the door itself are all sold separately. Pocket door frames can also be purchased as preassembled units that can be easily installed into a rough opening. Because C handles are used, the finished door opening will be 3 to 4 inches less than the same door with recessed hardware.

Framing and installing a pocket door is not difficult in new construction or a major remodel. But retrofitting a pocket door in place of a standard door, or installing one in a wall without an existing door, is a major project

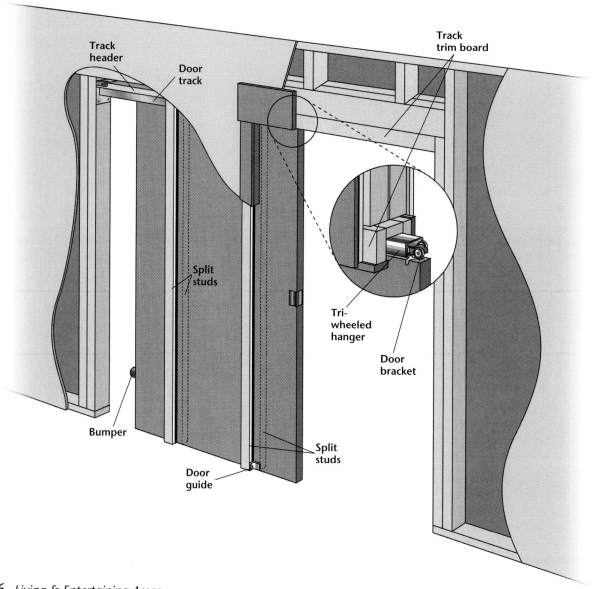

- Hammer
- Screwdriver
- Pry bar
- Reciprocating saw
- Measuring tape
- Studfinder
- Plumb bob
- Circular saw
- Utility knife
- Drill
- Drywall T-square
- 4-ft. level
- Power miter saw

- Nail set
- 2 × 4 & 2 × 6 lumber
- ½" plywood
- 8d, 10d & 16d nails
- Drywall panels
- 1¼" coarse-thread drywall screws
- All-purpose drywall compound
- Paper joint tape
- 6" & 12" drywall knives

- 150-grit sanding sponge
- Pocket door track and split studs
- Tapered wood shims
- C pull handles
- 4d & 6d finish nails
- Pocket door
- Split jambs
- Door casing

that involves removing the wall material, framing the new opening, installing and hanging the door, and refinishing the wall. Hidden utilities, such as wiring, plumbing, and heating ducts, must be rerouted if encountered.

The rough opening for a pocket door is at least twice the width of a standard door opening.

This project is for pocket door installation in a non-loadbearing wall. If the wall is loadbearing, it is recommended that you hire a contractor. If you are not sure whether the wall is loadbearing, consult a professional.

HOW TO INSTALL A POCKET DOOR IN A NON-LOADBEARING WALL

Prepare the rough door opening for the pocket door following steps A to C in "How to Widen an Interior Doorway" on pages 21 to 23. Make sure you frame the rough opening to the manufacturer's recommended dimensions. Even though the wall is non-loadbearing, the large size of the opening dictates using 2 × 6s sandwiched around ½" plywood for the header (step B, number 7 on page 23). Because you will be using C handles instead of recessed hardware, your door will need to be at least 36" wide to have the minimum 32" opening. Before beginning the door track installation, paint or stain the pocket door with the desired finish.

STEP A: *Cut the Track & Trim to Size*

1. Remove the adjustable end bracket from the overhead door track. Cut the wooden track header at the mark that matches your chosen door size. Turn the track over and cut the metal track 1⅜" shorter than the wooden track header, using a hacksaw.

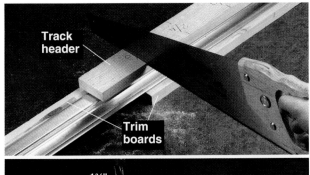

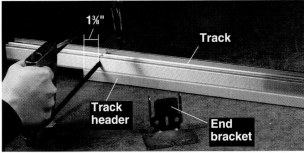

A. *Remove the end bracket and cut the track header to length (top). Use a hacksaw to cut the track to length (bottom).*

B. *Center the adjustable end bracket on the jack stud, level the track and set the nails.*

2. Replace the end bracket. Cut the side trim boards along the marks corresponding to your door size. Be careful not to cut the metal track (bottom).

STEP B: *Hang the Track*

1. Measuring from the floor, mark the center of each jack stud at the height of the door plus ¾" to 1½" (depending on the door clearance above the floor) for the overhead door track. Drive a nail into each jack stud, centered on the mark. Leave about ⅛" of the nail protruding.

2. Set the adjustable end brackets of the track on the nails in the jack studs.

3. Adjust the track to level and set the nails. Drive 8d common nails through the remaining holes in the end brackets.

STEP C: *Install the Split Studs*

1. Snap two chalk lines on the floor across the opening, even with the sides of the opening.

2. Tap floor plate spacers into the bottom ends of the pairs of steel-clad split studs.

3. Butt one split stud against the door track trim board, check it for plumb, and fasten it to the track header using 6d common nails.

4. Center the other split stud in the "pocket" and fasten it to the track header. Plumb the split studs

again and attach them to the floor with 8d common nails or 2" screws driven through the spacer plates.

STEP D: *Hang the Door*

1. Attach two door brackets to the top of the door, using the included screws driven through pilot holes. Install the rubber bumper to the rear edge of the door with its included screw.

2. Slide two tri-wheeled hangers into the overhead door track. Set the door in the frame, aligning the hangers with the door brackets.

3. Raise the door and press each hanger into the door bracket until it snaps into place. Close the lock arm over the hanger.

STEP E: *Install the Door Jambs*

1. Cut the strike-side jamb to length and width. Fasten it to the jack stud, using 8d casing nails. Shim the jamb to plumb if necessary.

2. Close the door and adjust the hanger nuts to fine-tune the door height so the door is parallel with the jamb from top to bottom.

3. Measure and cut the split jambs to size. Fasten each split jamb to the front edge of the split stud, using 8d finish nails. Maintain a ⅜₆" clearance on both sides of the door.

C. *Nail the split studs to the track header (left) and to the floor (right).*

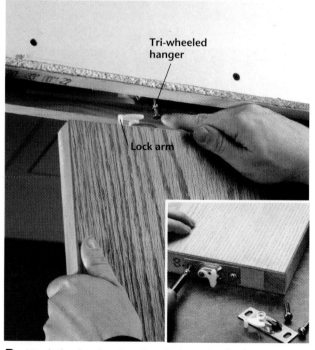

D. *Attach the door brackets (inset), then raise the door and press each hanger into the bracket.*

4. Measure and cut the split head jambs to size. Use 1½" wood screws driven through countersunk pilot holes to attach the head jamb on the side that has access to the lock arm of the hangers to allow for later removal or maintenance of the door. Attach the other head jamb using 6d finish nails. Maintain ³⁄₁₆" clearance on each side of the door.

STEP F: *Install Stop Blocks & C Handles*

1. Mount the C pull handles 1½" from the edge of the door. Slide the door closed until there is a 1½" space between the C pull and the door jamb.

2. At the back side of the frame, install a stop block to maintain the 1½" space between the C pull and the door jamb. Make sure the rubber bumper is hitting the stop block.

STEP G: *Install the Wallboard*

1. Install wallboard over the pocket to the edge of the opening, following the directions on page 23, step D. Use 1¼" wallboard screws that will not protrude into the pocket.

2. Tape and finish the wallboard, following steps D-F on pages 23 and 24.

STEP H: *Install the Casing*

1. Finish the new wallboard to match the old.

2. On the edge of each jamb, make short pencil marks about ⅛" from the inside edge—these setback marks represent the inside edges of the casing (see page 25). Mark at both ends of each jamb, and make sure the amount of setback remains consistent.

3. Place a length of casing along one side jamb so the bottom end is on the floor and the inside edge is aligned with the setback marks. At the top corner of the door frame, mark the point where the vertical and horizontal setback lines meet.

4. Miter-cut the casing at 45°. Tack the piece into place with two 4d finish nails driven through the casing and into the jamb. Drill pilot holes for nails to prevent splitting. Do not drive the nails flush.

5. Mark, cut, and tack up the casing on the other side of the door.

6. Cut the top casing piece to fit between the vertical pieces. Make sure it fits well, then drill pilot holes and drive 4d finish nails every 16". Drive 6d finish nails through the casing near the outer edge, into the wall framing. Drive all nail heads below the surface with a nail set. Fill nail holes with matching wood putty.

7. Reinstall the floor trim or baseboards.

E. *Fasten each split jamb to the front edge of the split stud (left). Use wood screws to attach the head jamb on the side that has access to the lock arms of the hanger (right).*

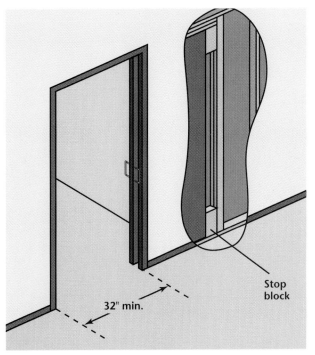

F. *Install a stop block at the back of the frame (right), so the door stops 1½" short of the C pulls. Make sure the rubber bumper hits the stop block.*

SWITCHES

Specialty switches make life easier and safer for the elderly or people with limited vision or mobility because they allow control of light intensity, automate on and off times, and connect a fixture to more than one control.

Replacing a switch is an easy project. Specialty switches available include rocker, dimmer, and motion- and sound-activated. All of these switches can be purchased as lighted versions. This makes them easier to locate in the dark, and makes them stand out for people with vision problems.

Rocker switches are a good choice when limited hand strength is an issue because they can be activated with a simple push.

Dimmer switches should be considered for people who suffer from light sensitivity because they adjust a light's intensity and reduce glare. Fluorescent light fixtures are not typically compatible with dimmer switches.

Motion- and sound-activated switches are helpful to people who use wheelchairs or walkers and for those with memory problems because they turn lights on and off automatically when someone enters or leaves the room.

The project detailed here shows replacing a toggle switch with a rocker switch, but most specialty switches will connect in a similar way.

IDENTIFYING SWITCH TYPES

When you go to purchase your new switch, you will need to know which type to buy. There are three standard types of wall switches: single-pole, three-way, and four-way—all are shown here. Each type can be identified by the number of screw terminals it has. Newer switches may also have push fittings in addition to screw terminals.

Most switches include a grounding terminal, which is identified by its green color. When pigtailed to the grounding wires, the grounding screw provides added protection against shock. If a switch doesn't have a grounding screw, it must be contained in a grounded metal electrical box.

Rocker　　**Lighted**　　**Dimmer**　　**Motion-sensor**

Single-pole Switches

A single-pole switch is the most common type of wall switch. It usually has ON-OFF markings on the switch lever, and is used to control a set of lights, an appliance, or a receptacle from a single location. A single-pole switch has two screw terminals. Most types also have a grounding screw.

A hot circuit wire is attached to each screw terminal. However, the color and number of wires inside the switch box vary, depending on the switch's location along the electrical circuit.

If two cables enter the box, the switch lies in the middle of the cable run (bottom left photo). In this installation, both of the hot wires attached to the switch are black.

If only one cable enters the box, the switch lies at the end of the cable run (bottom right photo). In this installation (sometimes called a *switch loop*), one of the hot wires is black, but the other is white. You should code a white hot wire with black tape or paint to identify it as hot.

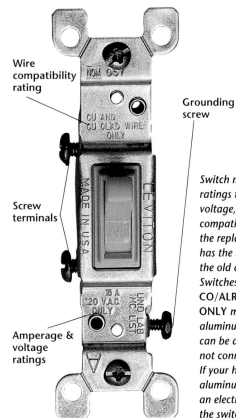

Wire compatibility rating

Grounding screw

Screw terminals

Amperage & voltage ratings

Switch markings indicate ratings for amperage, voltage, and wire compatibility. Make sure the replacement switch has the same ratings as the old device. Note: Switches marked CO/ALR or CU-CLAD ONLY may indicate aluminum wiring, which can be a fire hazard if not connected properly. If your house has aluminum wiring, hire an electrician to replace the switch.

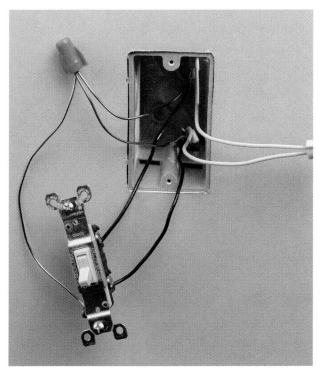

Installation of a single-pole switch in the middle of a cable run.

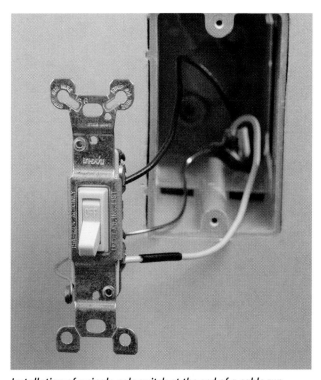

Installation of a single-pole switch at the end of a cable run.

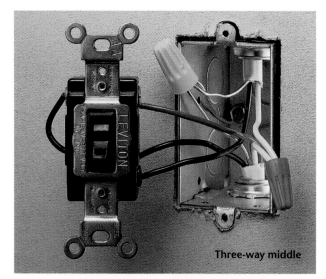

Three-way middle

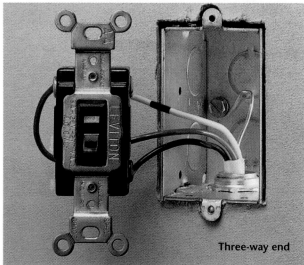

Three-way end

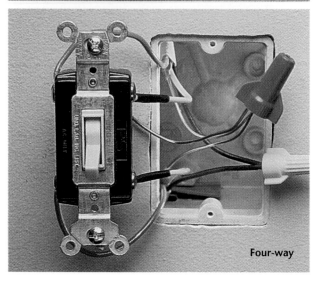

Four-way

Three-way Switches

Three-way switches have three screw terminals and do not have ON-OFF markings. They are always installed in pairs and are used to control a set of lights from two locations.

One screw terminal on the three-way switch is darker than the others. This is the common screw terminal; its position may vary by manufacturer. The two lighter-colored screw terminals are called traveler screw terminals. These terminals are interchangeable.

If a switch lies in the middle of a cable run (photo left, top), the box will have two cables: one 2-wire cable, and one 3-wire cable. The black (hot) wire from the 2-wire cable is connected to the common screw terminal, and the red and black wires from the 3-wire cable connect to the traveler terminals.

At the end of a cable run, a three-way switch is connected to one 3-wire cable (photo left, middle). The white wire is coded black for hot.

Four-way Switches

Four-way switches have four screw terminals and do not have ON-OFF markings. They are always installed between a pair of three-way switches to control a set of lights from three or more locations. Four-way switches are common in homes where large rooms contain multiple living areas, such as where a kitchen opens into a dining room.

In a typical four-way switch installation, a pair of 3-wire cables enters the switch box (photo left, bottom). With most switches, the hot wires from one cable attach to the bottom or top pair of screw terminals, and the hot wires from the other cable attach to the remaining pair of screw terminals. However, wiring configurations may vary by manufacturer. Consult the wiring diagram provided with the switch. Some four-way switches have a wiring guide stamped on the back of the device.

HOW TO REPLACE A TOGGLE SWITCH WITH A ROCKER SWITCH

STEP A: *Pull Out the Old Switch*

1. Turn off the power to the switch at the main service panel.

2. Remove the switch coverplate and the mounting screws holding the switch to the electrical box. Be careful not to touch any bare wires or screw terminals until you check the switch for power. Carefully pull the switch from the box by holding the mounting straps.

STEP B: *Test the Switch for Power*

1. Test the switch for power by touching one probe of a neon circuit tester to the grounded metal box or the bare copper grounding wire, and touch the other probe to each screw terminal of the switch.

The tester should not glow. If it does, return to the service panel and turn off the correct circuit.

2. Disconnect the circuit wires and remove the switch.

STEP C: *Install the New Switch*

1. Inspect the bare ends of the circuit wires. If they are broken or nicked, clip off the damaged portion, using a combination tool, then strip the insulation so there is about ¾" of bare wire at the end of each wire. Clean darkened or dirty wire ends with fine sandpaper.

2. Connect the circuit wires to the screw terminals on the rocker switch, following the manufacturer's wiring diagram (the white wire shown here is marked with black tape to indicate that it is hot). Tighten the screws firmly, but avoid overtightening, which may strip the screw threads.

3. Carefully tuck the wires inside the box and mount the switch to the electrical box, using the mounting screws. Install the switch coverplate.

4. Restore power to the switch at the main service panel.

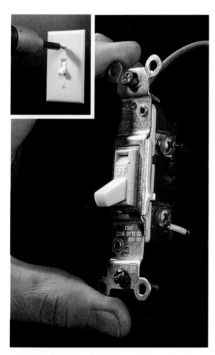

A. *Remove the switch coverplate (inset). Remove the mounting screws and carefully pull the old switch from the box.*

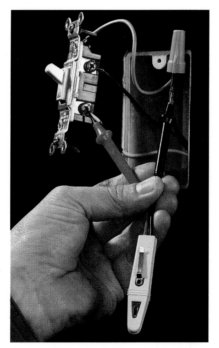

B. *Test the switch for power, using a neon circuit tester.*

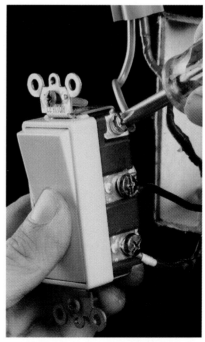

C. *Install the new rocker switch, following the manufacturer's wiring diagram.*

TRACK LIGHTING

Track lighting enhances safety by directing light to brighten work areas and eliminate glare and shadows for people with limited vision.

Track lighting kits are available at most home improvement stores. They come in a variety of styles, so you can mix and match components to get what you need. Installation is easy because the entire system can be powered from a single electrical box. The first track mounts over the box and is connected to the circuit wiring. Additional tracks are mounted to the ceiling and are tied into the first track with L- or T-connectors.

When determining where to install the tracks, don't limit yourself to the ceiling. Track systems on walls make it easier for wheelchair and walker users to reach the fixtures for repositioning and bulb replacement. Lower placement can also produce more effective task lighting.

Take a look at your room's layout and power sources. It's easiest to install track lighting in place of an existing light fixture. If no wiring is currently in place where you will need it, hire a licensed electrician to install a new electrical cable and box to accomodate the track lighting. Because fixtures vary, always follow the manufacturer's installation instructions.

TOOLS & MATERIALS

- Tape measure
- Neon circuit tester
- Screwdrivers
- Straightedge
- Pencil
- Track lighting kit
- Drill
- Wire connectors
- Toggle bolts

HOW TO INSTALL TRACK LIGHTS
STEP A: *Remove the Old Fixture & Install the Power Supply Connector*
1. At the main service panel, turn off the power to the circuit you'll be working on.

A. *Join the power supply connector to the circuit wires with wire connectors.*

2. When you're sure the power is off, disconnect the wires for the old fixture and remove it.

3. Connect the power supply connector by joining the green ground wire to the bare copper circuit wire with a wire connector. If required, connect a grounding pigtail to the electrical box.

4. Attach the white connector wire to the white circuit wire, and attach the connector's black wire to the black circuit wire.

5. Carefully tuck the wires into the electrical box, then secure the connector's mounting plate to the box with screws.

STEP B: *Mount the First Track*

1. Use a pencil and straightedge to mark the position of the first track leading from the electrical box. If possible, position tracks underneath ceiling joists to provide backing for screws.

2. Snap the first track onto the mounting plate and secure it to the tab with a screw.

3. Loosely fasten the remainder of the track with screws driven into ceiling joists. Where there's no backing, use toggle bolts to secure the track to the ceiling surface. Leave all fasteners loose until all of

the track pieces are hung.

STEP C: *Mount Power Supply Connector & Connect the Remaining Tracks*

1. Insert the power supply connector into the track and twist it into position, following the manufacturer's instructions.

2. Attach the power supply cover.

3. Using L-connectors for corners and T-connectors to join three tracks, connect and mount the remaining tracks one at a time. Loosely fasten the tracks to the ceiling.

4. After all of the tracks are in place, tighten all of the fasteners. Close open ends of track with dead-end pieces.

STEP D: *Install the Fixtures*

1. Insert the lighting fixtures into the tracks and twist-lock them into place in the desired positions. Install lightbulbs in the fixtures.

2. Turn on power to the circuit at the main service panel. Switch on the power to the track lighting, and adjust the beams for the desired effect.

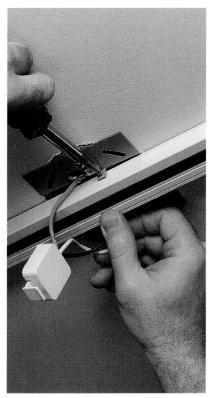

B. *Screw the first track to the mounting plate, then loosely fasten it to the ceiling.*

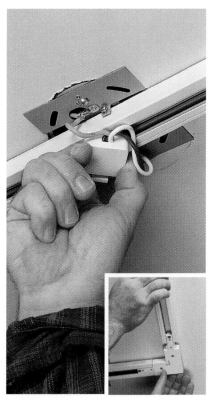

C. *Attach the power supply connector. Join tracks with L- or T-connectors (inset).*

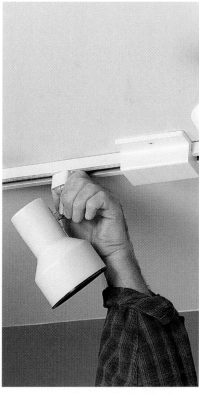

D. *Install the fixtures into the tracks, add bulbs, then adjust the fixture positions.*

KITCHENS

The kitchen is the heart of the home. It's the emotional center where the family gathers to share good food and special details of the day. An accessible kitchen invites everyone to the table for the socialization, creativity, and empowerment that accompanies cooking and dining.

There are many simple ways to make your current kitchen serve your family better. Under-cabinet lighting can illuminate the countertop for a cook with limited vision. Glide-out, pull-down, and swing-up shelves can bring heavy appliances and bowls to a cook with limited mobility or strength. And a new kitchen faucet with a scald-prevention device and lever handle can make cleanup safer and easier for a cook with nerve damage or limited hand strength.

If you want to build a kitchen from the ground up, you'll find ideas for cabinets, countertops, appliances, and kitchen design that will serve accessibility, as well as your sense of beauty and style.

Photo courtesy of IKEA.

Flooring

Since most kitchen work is performed while standing, choose cushioned flooring materials, such as cork or vinyl, to minimize leg fatigue for the elderly or people with back or leg injuries. To increase safety, choose a nonslip, matte finish that reduces glare and prevents falls.

Neutral colors help reduce eyestrain, and adding a contrasting border around the room's edge can help people with vision problems mark boundaries.

■ **Wheelchair Modifications:**

• Choose durable flooring with a nonslip, glare-free finish that can withstand wheel tracking.

Cabinetry

Reorganize kitchen cabinets to put everyday items within easy reach. Move plates, cups, and glasses to base cabinets, or use countertop accessories, such as plate racks and appliance garages, for everyday dishes.

Include a swing-out stool under the sink so family members with back or leg problems can sit while doing the dishes or cleaning vegetables.

If cabinets are too high or too deep, add glide-out, pull-down, and pop-up shelves to eliminate reaching and bending.

Replace knobs with magnetic touch latches or C-shaped handles so people with limited hand strength can open cabinets with a simple push or pull.

■ **Wheelchair Modifications:**

• Replace standard drawer slides with full-extension hardware to eliminate reaching.

• Remove toekicks on standard base cabinets, or raise them to 8".

• Install bifold, fold-out, or removable doors on base cabinets, and remove face frames to open up sitting areas.

• Include at least one rolling base cabinet that can be moved away to create a sitting area at the countertop.

• Install base cabinets at various heights: 30 to 32" for seated users; 36" for standing users; and 42" for tall users. Or hang an adjustable-height cabinet that can be manually or electronically adjusted for various users.

• Hang some sections of upper cabinets at 12 to 15" above the countertop for easier seated access.

Kitchen cabinets with removable sections (left) allow you to make changes as you need them. Adjustable-height cabinets and sinks (above) bring items within reach.

Design your kitchen around a clear, circular space of at least 5 ft. in diameter to provide room for a wheelchair. If your kitchen doesn't have 60" of clear space, allow 48" for pathways. Plan for 30 to 48" of clear approach space in front of all appliances and workstations.

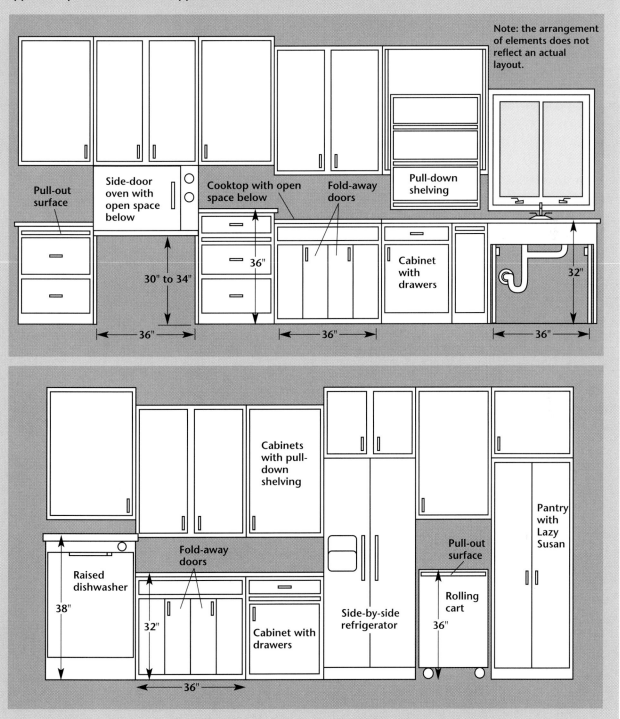

Note: the arrangement of elements does not reflect an actual layout.

Pull-out surface

Side-door oven with open space below

Cooktop with open space below

Fold-away doors

Pull-down shelving

30" to 34"

36"

Cabinet with drawers

32"

36"

36"

36"

Cabinets with pull-down shelving

Raised dishwasher

38"

Fold-away doors

Cabinet with drawers

32"

Side-by-side refrigerator

Pull-out surface

Rolling cart

36"

Pantry with Lazy Susan

36"

Countertops

Create a continuous work surface between the sink and the stove so people with limited arm strength can slide heavy pots instead of lifting them. Include an area of heat-resistant countertop near the stove to accept pans moved directly from a burner.

When replacing countertops, look for a spill-proof lip to keep floors safe for people with limited mobility, and select a contrasting edge to help people with vision problems identify boundaries. Select special features, such as cutouts, to help people with limited hand strength hold mixing bowls.

■ Wheelchair Modifications:

• Add pull-out sections of countertop to create roll-under workspace.

• Include at least one section of countertop at 32". Or install an adjustable-height countertop, which can be set for various users.

Appliances

Install or raise appliances at convenient heights. Raising your dishwasher 6" and installing your microwave oven at countertop height (32") will allow people with back or mobility problems to reach them more easily. Use pop-up shelves to keep heavy mixers, juicers, or breadmakers accessible but out of the way.

Opt for a separate oven and cooktop. A wall-mounted oven installed at 30 to 34" and a counter-level cooktop installed no higher than 32", instead of a combination stove and oven, will make cooking safer and easier. Choose

Contrasting edges on countertops create visual interest in the kitchen, and they help people with vision problems mark boundaries.

Photo courtesy of Dura Supreme.

Recessed lighting provides soft, ambient lighting. Combine it with task lighting to reduce or eliminate glare and shadows.

staggered burners and front-mounted controls that eliminate reaching and allow a cook to work while seated. Wall-mounted ovens are available with side-swinging doors, which eliminates reaching over a hot oven door.

When replacing appliances, look for features that serve people with disabilities. For example, a side-by-side refrigerator, a drawer-style dishwasher, or a front-loading washer and dryer can benefit people with limited mobility.

Water and ice dispensers, or automated appliances that offer hands-free operation, can help people with limited hand strength.

Radiant or halogen cooktops that glow when hot, or magnetic induction cooktops that remain cool while they cook, are helpful to people with vision problems.

■ Wheelchair Modifications:

• Raise the dishwasher 6", or consider a drawer-style model for easier access.

• Lower the microwave to countertop height of 32" or install it below the countertop if there will be no standing users.

• Choose a cooktop with front- or side-mounted controls, positioned less than 21" from the front of the counter, and install it with 32 to 36" of clear space below for roll- under access.

• Insulate the underside of the cooktop to prevent burns, and add bifold, fold-back, or removable doors to hide roll-under space when not in use.

• Attach a non-fog mirror over the cooktop, so seated cooks can see into pots at the rear of the stove.

• Install a range hood with front- or counter-mounted controls.

• Wall-mount the oven at 30 to 34", and choose a side-swing door.

• Purchase a side-by-side refrigerator to put fresh and frozen food at eye level, and add a second, small refrigerator near the eating area to eliminate trips to the kitchen.

• Choose a front-loading, side-by-side washer and dryer so seated users can see inside the machines.

A side-swing, wall-mounted oven puts food at eye level and reduces bending and reaching for wheelchair users and young family members.

Cooktops with front-mounted controls and fold-away doors on base cabinets provide roll-under access for wheelchair users.

Sinks

Install a scald-guard valve on your kitchen faucet to protect people with slow reflexes or nerve damage from sudden changes in water temperature.

If limited hand strength is an issue, change double-handled faucets to single-lever styles, or install sensor-activated faucets for hands-free operation.

Add a sprayer hose to the sink to help people with back problems or limited arm strength fill pots without needing to lift them out of the sink. Newer models incorporate the sprayer into the spout.

A hot water dispenser installed at the sink so coffee, tea, and soup can be prepared without turning on the stove is convenient for elderly family members.

If you're remodeling a kitchen consider the depth of the sink and the placement of the faucets. A shallow sink may be easier to use and

A kitchen sprayer makes cleanup easy and helps eliminate lifting when used to convieniently fill pots outside the sink.

faucets can be placed at the sink side rather than the back.

■ Wheelchair Modifications:

• Install an adjustable-height sink, or mount the kitchen sink at 32". Remove face frames on base cabinets, or include bifold, fold-out, or removable doors to create roll-under access. Add an appearance panel or insulate sink pipes beneath to protect family members from burns.

• Choose a sink that is 6" or less in depth to eliminate reaching and allow more knee space.

Lighting/Electrical

Reduce glare for the elderly and people with vision problems by adding anti-glare films to kitchen windows.

Use recessed fixtures and full-spectrum lightbulbs that imitate sunlight and eliminate shadows. For people with mobility problems, choose long-life bulbs that require less-frequent replacement and install automated window shade openers.

Use spotlights to illuminate task areas, such as kitchen

Install a tilted mirror above the cooktop so seated cooks can see into pots without reaching.

desks or islands, and add under-cabinet lighting to brighten countertops. Under-cabinet fixtures can double as nightlights to make kitchen visits safer for the elderly and people with limited mobility.

Install lighted rocker switches to help people with limited hand strength or vision problems locate and operate lights more easily at night. Or, install motion-detector switches which turn lights on automatically when someone enters the room.

Replace any standard electrical receptacles with ground-fault circuit-interrupters (GFCIs) to prevent electrical shock.

■ **Wheelchair Modifications:**

• Install countertop electrical receptacles no more than 21" from the front edge of the countertop.

• Replace standard light switches with motion-sensor or voice-activated switches.

Use spotlights to illuminate islands and work stations.

A well-lit kitchen is both beautiful and safe. Use a combination of lighting styles to brighten the kitchen during the day and to provide warm, ambient light at night.

UNDER-CABINET LIGHTING

Under-cabinet lighting puts light right on the countertop, benefiting people with vision problems. When these fixtures double as nightlights, they also enhance nighttime kitchen safety for the elderly and people with limited mobility.

There are many styles of under-cabinet lights available. You'll find rope lights, strip lights, mini-tracks, halogen lights, and incandescent lights. Fluorescent styles are the most popular because they combine excellent lighting with energy efficiency, and they remain cool—unlike some other types.

If you need extra light in only one area, a simple plug-in fixture may suit your needs. When you want to install several units, however, hard-wired fixtures are a better option. Installation is simple and usually does not require an electrician.

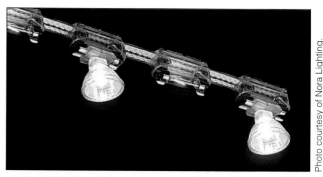

Undercabinet lighting comes in a variety of styles to fit your lighting needs in every room of the house. There are rope lights, strip lights, and mini-tracks with incandescent, halogen, and fluorescent bulbs.

Photo courtesy of Nora Lighting.

The project shown here is for a set of hard-wired under-cabinet fluorescent lights with a wall switch. Units are attached under upper-cabinet bases and are wired through the wall with a few simple connections. Make sure the wattage of your new lights does not exceed the safe capacity of your circuit.

To adjust a fixture that creates glare or is too bright for people sitting nearby, try positioning lights either farther back or to the front of the upper-cabinet base. You can also install an opaque glass cover over your fixtures, add a shield under the upper cabinets, or install a larger cabinet facing to reduce glare.

Consult your local electrical inspector about cable requirements in your area and the power source from which you may draw. In some areas, codes require armored cable, and you may be prohibited from drawing power from a receptacle, as shown in this project.

TOOLS & MATERIALS

- Neon circuit tester
- Utility knife
- Hammer
- Screwdriver
- Drill & bits
- Combination tool
- Under-cabinet lighting kit

- 12-2 NM cable
- Cable clamps
- Pigtail wiring
- Twist-on wire connectors
- Plastic switch box
- Switch

HOW TO INSTALL UNDER-CABINET LIGHTING

STEP A: *Prepare the Installation Area*

1. Shut off the power to the receptacle you plan to draw power from, then use a neon circuit tester to confirm that the power is off (see page 33).

2. Disconnect the receptacle from its wiring.

3. Mark and cut a channel to route the cable, using a utility knife. (To make the drywall repair easier after the installation, we cut a 6"-tall channel in the center of the installation area.)

STEP B: *Install the Switch Box & Cable*

1. Drill holes through the cabinet edging and/or the wall surface directly beneath the cabinets where the cable will enter each light fixture. Drill ⅝" holes through the studs for running the cable. The front edges of the holes should be at least 1¼" back from the front stud edges.

2. Install a plastic switch box by nailing it to the stud with preinstalled nails.

3. Route a length of 12-2 cable from the switch box to the receptacle box.

4. Route another cable from the switch box to the first fixture hole.

5. If you are installing more than one set of lights, route cables from the first fixture location to the second, and so on.

STEP C: *Make the Connections*

1. Clamp the switch-to-receptacle cable into the receptacle box with 8" extending into the box. Strip the sheathing from the cable end (see page 46).

2. Connect the switch cable and power source cable to the receptacle, using twist-on wire connectors. Pigtail the white wires to the silver terminal on the receptacle, and pigtail the black wires to the brass terminal. Pigtail the grounding wires to the grounding screw in the electrical box.

3. Tuck the wiring into the box and reattach the receptacle.

STEP D: *Attach & Connect the Light Fixtures*

1. Remove the access cover, lens, and bulb from the light fixture.

2. Open the knockouts for running the cables into the fixture. Insert the cables and secure them with cable clamps.

3. Strip 8" of sheathing from the cables, then attach the fixture to the bottom of the cabinet with screws.

4. Use wire connectors to join the black, white, and ground leads from the light fixture to each of

A. *Remove the receptacle from the source cable, then cut a channel for the cable.*

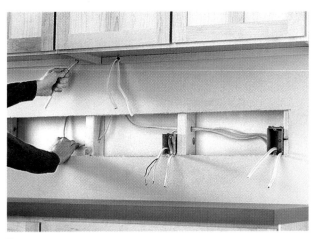

B. *Install a new switch box and route cable to the power source and fixture.*

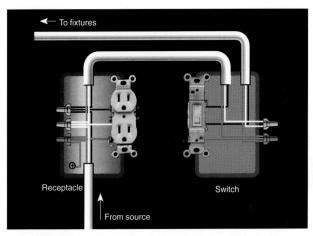

C. *Use pigtails to connect the source cable and switch cable to the receptacle.*

the corresponding cable wires from the wall, including any cable leading to additional fixtures.

5. Reattach the bulb, lens, and access cover to the fixture.

6. Install and connect any additional fixtures.

STEP E: *Wire the Switch*

1. Clamp the cables into the switch box with 8" extending into the box. Strip the sheathing from the two cable ends.

2. Join the white wires together with wire connectors. Connect each black wire to a screw terminal on the switch. Pigtail the grounding wires to the grounding screw on the switch.

3. Install the switch and coverplate, and restore power to the circuit.

4. Patch any removed drywall (page 23).

D. *Install the fixtures and connect them to the branch cables.*

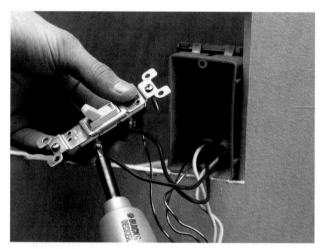

E. *Make the connections at the switch, then install the switch and coverplate and restore power.*

WORKING WITH WIRE

Cut the plastic sheathing on nonmetallic cable using a utility knife or cable ripper. Peel back the sheathing and paper wrapping from the individual wires.

Strip insulation for each wire using an electrician's combination tool. Choose the stripper opening that matches the wire gauge. Take care not to nick or scratch the ends of the wire. Strip ¾" of insulation from each wire.

Connect wires to screw termininals by hooking each wire around the screw terminal so it forms a clockwise loop. Tighten the screw firmly. The insulation should just touch the head of the screw.

Use a pigtail to connect two or more wires to a single screw terminal.

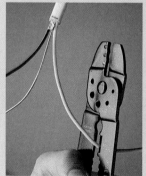

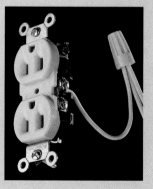

GLIDE-OUT, PULL-DOWN & SWING-UP SHELVES

Eliminate bending, reaching, and lifting for people with limited mobility or arm strength by incorporating a few simple accessories into standard kitchen cabinetry.

An entire industry has been built around specialized shelving and hardware, making it easier than ever to customize your kitchen storage with pull-down, swing-up, and glide-out shelves.

Choose pull-down shelf accessories to bring upper-cabinet items like spices within reach. Incorporate heavy-duty, swing-up shelves to bring base-cabinet items like stand mixers to the countertop. Build your own full-extension, glide-out shelves to divide larger spaces into two or more shelves and reduce bending and reaching for wheelchair users and people with back problems.

Glide-out shelves

Swing-up shelves

Pull-down shelves

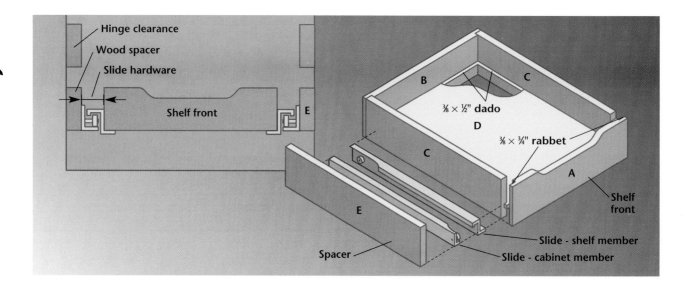

Labels in diagram: Hinge clearance, Wood spacer, Slide hardware, Shelf front, E, B, C, ⅜ × ½" dado, D, ⅜ × ¾" rabbet, A, C, Shelf front, E, Spacer, Slide - shelf member, Slide - cabinet member

When purchasing specialized hardware accessories, check load ratings, locking mechanisms, arc swings, and clearance heights to be sure they can support the items you want to store and they will fit in the intended location. You may have to add spacers to provide enough clearance for the hardware to slide past your cabinet's hinges or face frame. Also be aware that many swing arms are sold without the shelf surface, which must be cut to fit or purchased separately.

Take accurate measurements of your cabinet's interior dimensions, note any objects that protrude into the interior, and purchase specialized hardware that is compatible with your cabinetry. Frameless cabinets often have fully concealed hinges that can interfere with swing mechanisms. Framed cabinets will have a front perimeter face frame and may have hinges that

Key	Part	Dimension
A	(1) Shelf front	¾ × 3 × 26" hardwood
B	(1) Shelf back	¾ × 3 × 26" hardwood
C	(1) Shelf side	¾ × 3 × 22¼" hardwood
D	(1) Shelf bottom	½ × 25¼ × 22¼" plywood
E	(2) Spacer	¾ × 3 × 22¼" hardwood

TOOLS & MATERIALS

- Jig saw
- Router with bits
- Hammer
- Clamps
- Drill with bits
- Nail set
- Circular saw
- Straightedge guide
- Finishing sander
- 4d finish nails
- (2) Drawer guides
- Finishing materials
- 1¼" utility screws
- Level
- Screwdriver
- Wood glue

½" dado

A. *Rout dado and rabbet grooves in the 1 × 3.*

interfere with lift and glide hardware.

HOW TO INSTALL GLIDE-OUT SHELVES
STEP A: *Cut the Shelf Pieces & Rout the Joints*
1. Determine the size of the glide-out shelves by measuring the inside dimensions of the cabinet and subtracting the distance any objects protrude into the interior of the cabinet (hinges and face frames). Then subtract 1" from the width for the two slides and tracks (½" each).

2. Cut the front (A) and back (B) pieces for each shelf to the determined width. Then use a jig saw to cut out the top edge of the front pieces, making a decorative drawer pull area.

3. Determine the depth of the shelves by measuring the depth of the cabinet and subtracting 1". Cut the side pieces (C) for the shelves at this length.

4. Determine the width of the spacers (E), if they are necessary, and cut them to length so they fit along the interior walls of the cabinet.

5. Cut the bottom pieces (D) to size from ½" plywood.

6. Rout a ⅜"-deep × ½"-wide dado groove into the front, back, and side panels, ½" from the bottom edges using a straightedge guide.

7. Cut a ⅜"-deep × ¾"-wide rabbet groove across the inside faces of each end of the front and back pieces.

STEP B: *Assemble the Shelves*
1. Spread glue onto the rabbets of the shelf fronts and attach the sides using three 4d finishing nails to hold each joint. Countersink the nails with a nail set.

2. Slide the bottom panels into the dado grooves, then glue and nail the back pieces in place. Clamp the shelves square, letting the glue dry.

3. Smooth all surfaces with a finishing sander and 120-grit sandpaper. Wipe off all dust, then paint or varnish the shelf.

STEP C: *Mount the Drawer Glides*
1. Mount the glide-out rails to the bottom edges of the spacer strips (E). Then attach the spacers to the interior walls of the cabinet with 1¼" utility screws. Use a level to ensure the rails are installed properly.

2. Screw a sliding rail to each side of the shelves, making sure that the bottom edges of the glides are flush against the bottom edges of the shelves.

3. Install each shelf by aligning its sliding rails with the glides inside the cabinet and pushing it in completely. The rails will automatically lock into place.

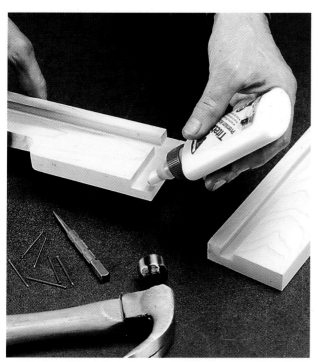

B. *Apply glue to the rabbet joints and nail the front pieces of the shelves to the sides.*

C. *Mount the glide-out rails on the spacer strips, then align the spacers with a level and screw them into the cabinet interior.*

TOOLS & MATERIALS

- Measuring tape
- Circular saw
- Drill & bits
- Pull-down shelf unit and installation hardware
- Wood finishing materials

- Wood for shelf
- #6 × ⅝" & #8 × ⅝" machine screws
- Coarse-thread drywall screws
- Lumber for spacers

HOW TO INSTALL A POP-UP SHELF

STEP A: *Test the Swing Arms & Cut the Spacers*

1. Carefully trigger the locking mechanism on each swing arm and set the arm in its fully extended position. Hold each arm against the inside face of the cabinet side and make sure the arm will clear the door hinge and/or the cabinet face frame. If the arms do not clear, you'll need to use wood spacers to allow the arms to clear the hinges or frames by at least ½". In most cases, one 1 × 3 spacer for each arm will provide enough clearance.

2. Cut the spacers so they match the length of the mounting plate on the swing arms.

STEP B: *Install the Swing Arms*

1. Following the manufacturer's instructions, mark the swing arm locations onto the inside faces of the cabinet sides. Use a straightedge to extend the height mark so it represents the full length of the spacer or mounting plate. Make sure the marks are identical on both cabinet sides so the arms will be level with each other. Make sure the prescribed clearances between the shelf and countertop will be met.

2. Carefully trigger the locking mechanism and rotate the swing arms into their fully retracted positions.

3. *If you are not using spacers:* Position each swing arm on its location marks and fasten it to the cabinet side with #8 machine screws. The screw length depends on the thickness of the cabinet side. The screws should not go completely through the cabinet side.

If you are using spacers: Position each spacer so its top and front edges are on the location marks, and fasten it to the cabinet side with coarse-thread drywall screws. The screw length depends on the thickness of the spacer and cabinet side. The

A. *Check the clearance of the swing arms. If necessary, measure for a spacer, using a measuring tape or a block as a gauge.*

B. *Mark the locations of the swing arm mounting plates onto the inside cabinet faces. Mount the swing arms with screws.*

screws should not go completely through the cabinet side. Using #8 machine screws, fasten the swing arms to the spacers so that the top edges of the mounting plate are flush with the top edge of the spacer and the front ends are flush.

STEP C: *Cut & Install the Shelf*

1. Unlock and rotate both swing arms so they are fully extended. Determine the width of the shelf by measuring across the swing arms, parallel to the countertop, and finding the distance between the outer edges of the shelf mounting flanges (on the ends of the swing arms). Refer to the manufacturer's recommendations for the proper length of the shelf to ensure it will fit into the cabinet when the assembly is locked down and the door is closed.

2. Cut the shelf from ¾"-thick plywood, MDF, or melamine-coated particleboard. If the shelf is bare wood, lightly sand the edges and finish all sides with a highly washable paint or a clear varnish, such as polyurethane. For melamine-coated board, cover the cut edges with melamine tape to prevent water from damaging the wood core.

3. Attach the shelf to the shelf mounting flanges using #8 machine screws. Follow the manufacturer's instructions for shelf placement.

STEP D: *Add the Locking Bars*

1. The locking bars provide you with fingertip control of the shelf locking mechanisms. Install them on the bottom face of the shelf. Next to each swing arm, position a locking bar so that its raised end lays over the shelf mounting flange and underneath the tab of the locking mechanism. The front end of the bar should be close to, or flush with, the front shelf edge.

2. Fasten each locking bar to the bottom shelf face with the provided screws and plastic spacers to ensure the bars will slide smoothly. Test the locking bars' operation with the shelf in the extended and retracted positions, and make any necessary adjustments.

3. If desired, attach the provided appliance spacers to the top of the shelf. These help keep the appliance in place on the shelf. Fasten the spacer to the shelf with the provided screws.

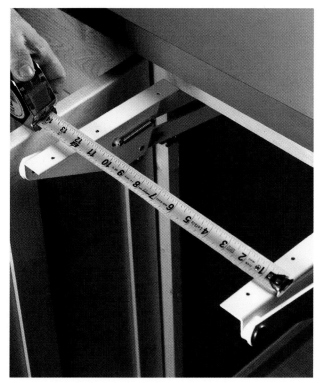

C. *Measure across the swing arms to find the shelf width. Cut the shelf to size and finish any bare surfaces.*

D. *Position the locking bars underneath the shelf and fasten them, using machine screws and plastic spacers.*

TOOLS & MATERIALS

- Tape measure
- Pencil
- Circular saw
- Drill & bits
- Awl
- Hacksaw
- Allen wrench

- Swing-up shelf kit & hardware
- ½" board for shelf boxes
- Fasteners & finishing materials for shelf boxes

- #8 pan-head screws
- Coarse-thread drywall screws
- Lumber for custom spacers (if needed)

HOW TO INSTALL A PULL-DOWN SHELF UNIT
STEP A: *Check the Clearances*

1. Using the wood spacer provided, hold each swing arm assembly against the inside face of the cabinet side and make sure both arms will clear the door hinge and the cabinet face frame. If the arms do not clear, add custom wood spacers of an adequate thickness. Some cabinets may not need spacers.

2. If you need to make custom spacers, cut pieces of plywood or solid lumber that are at least as large as the swing arm mounting plates. Using the man-ufacturer's paper template to determine the general positions of the swing arms (step B), fasten the spacers to the inside faces of the cabinet sides with coarse-thread drywall screws. The screw length depends on the thickness of the spacer and cabinet side. The screws should not go completely through the cabinet side.

STEP B: *Mark the Screw Holes & Install the Swing Arms*

1. Mark the screw hole positions for the swing arm mounting plates, using the manufacturer's template. Hold the template flat against each cabinet side and position it using the template's guide arrows. Use an awl to mark the screw hole centers onto the spacer or cabinet side. Drill a small pilot hole at each awl mark, making sure you don't drill completely through the cabinet side.

2. Position each swing arm assembly so the screw holes on the mounting plate align with the pilot holes (include the manufacturer's spacers, if you're using them). Fasten the swing arms to the custom spacers or cabinet sides with #8 pan-head screws. The screw length depends on the thickness of the cabinet side. The screws should not go completely through the cabinet side.

A. *Test the swing arms for clearance. If necessary, install a custom spacer block at the mounting plate locations.*

B. *Mark the screw holes with the manufacturer's template, drill pilot holes, then install the swing arms with screws (inset).*

STEP C: *Build & Install the Shelf Boxes*

1. Build two shelf boxes from ½"-thick plywood, MDF, or melamine-coated particleboard. Follow the manufacturer's specifications for the box dimensions, which will be based on the size of your cabinet. If the boxes are bare wood, lightly sand the edges and finish all sides with a highly washable paint or a clear varnish, such as polyurethane. For melamine-coated board, cover the cut edges with melamine tape, to keep water from damaging the wood core.

2. Install the boxes between the sides of the shelf unit, using the predrilled holes in the side pieces. Secure the boxes with #8 pan-head screws. Because the lower box can be installed in only one position, install it first. Then, find the desired position for the upper box, and secure it in place.

3. Slide the lower handle through the holes in the side pieces. Mark the handle to length so it projects ½" beyond the side piece on both sides. Cut the handle, using a hacksaw, and slide it through the side pieces so it overhangs an equal amount on both sides. Secure each end of the handle with a metal collar and setscrew, using an Allen wrench.

STEP D: *Complete the Assembly*

1. Determine the length of the top handle by measuring the distance between the outsides of the upper arms on the swing arm assemblies. Cut the upper handle to length, using a hacksaw.

2. With the assistance of a helper, position the box unit in front of the cabinet, rotate the lower arms down, and secure them to the side pieces using the bolts, washers, and nuts provided.

3. Insert the top handle through the holes at the top of the side pieces. With a helper, lower the upper arms down one at a time, and insert the handle end into the arm. Secure the handle with the two setscrews in each arm using an Allen wrench.

NOTE: In some units the springs that help raise the arms are quite strong and may make it slightly difficult to lower the shelves when they are empty. When the shelves are loaded, the weight of the items will make it easier to lower and raise the shelf.

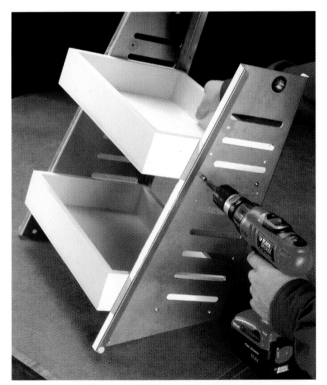

C. *Build the shelf boxes to fit between the shelf unit sides. Finish and install the boxes, then add the lower handle.*

D. *Connect the lower arms to the side pieces, then secure the upper arms to the upper handle.*

KITCHEN FAUCETS

Make the kitchen sink more accessible for people with limited strength or diminished nerve sensation, by installing a single-lever faucet that can be pushed on and off, fitted with a scald-guard device, and adapted with an extra-long sprayer hose to fill pots on the countertop.

Replacing a faucet is a simple project that can update your kitchen and improve safety immediately. Single-lever faucets are available in a variety of styles, including double-lever models that offer traditional styling. Choose a separate pull-out sprayer or an incorporated sprayer that pulls out from the spout, then springs back into place after use.

Fit your new faucet with a scald-guard valve to protect family members against sudden changes in water temperature. Temperature-limiting mixer valves also prevent scalds by restricting water temperature at one faucet.

To protect your family at every faucet in the house, turn down your hot water heater's thermostat. Make sure, however, that the setting stays at least at 130° for health reasons.

To get the maximum benefit, choose a faucet that includes all three features—lever handle,

Photo courtesy of Elkay.

TOOLS & MATERIALS

- Basin wrench or channel-type pliers
- Putty knife
- Caulk gun
- Adjustable wrenches

- Penetrating oil
- Silicone caulk or plumber's putty
- Two flexible supply tubes

pull-out sprayer, and scald-guard device—as shown in this project.

HOW TO INSTALL A SINGLE-LEVER FAUCET WITH SCALD GUARD AND SINK SPRAYER

STEP A: *Remove the Old Faucet*

1. Turn off the water to the faucet.

2. Spray penetrating oil on the tailpiece mounting nuts and supply tube coupling nuts.

3. Remove the coupling nuts and the tailpiece mounting nuts with a basin wrench or channel-type pliers.

4. Remove the faucet, and use a putty knife to clean away old putty from the surface of the sink.

STEP B: *Install the New Faucet*

1. Apply a ¼" bead of silicone caulk or plumber's putty around the base of the new faucet.

A. *Spray penetrating oil on the tailpiece mounting nuts and supply tube coupling nuts, then use channel-type pliers or a basin wrench to remove the nuts (inset).*

2. Insert the faucet tailpieces into the sink openings, positioning the faucet so the base is parallel to the back of the sink.

3. Press the faucet down to form a good seal with the caulk.

STEP C: *Attach the Supply Tubes*

1. Screw the metal friction washers and the mounting nuts onto the tailpieces, then tighten them with a basin wrench or channel-type pliers. Wipe away excess caulk around the base of the faucet.

2. Connect the flexible supply tubes to the faucet tailpieces. Tighten the coupling nuts with a basin wrench or channel-type pliers.

3. Attach the supply tubes to the shutoff valves, using compression fittings. Hand-tighten the nuts, then use an adjustable wrench to tighten the nuts ¼ turn. If necessary, hold the valve with another wrench while tightening.

B. *Apply a ¼" bead of silicone caulk or plumber's putty around the base of the new faucet.*

C. *Screw the metal friction washers and mounting nuts onto the tailpieces and tighten them with a basin wrench or channel-type pliers.*

FAUCET HOOKUP VARIATIONS

New Faucet without Supply Tubes: Buy two supply tubes. Supply tubes are available in braided steel or vinyl mesh (shown at left), PB plastic (acceptable by most codes for exposed supply lines), or chromed copper.

New Faucet with Preattached Tubing: Make water connections by attaching the supply tubing directly to the shutoff valves with compression fittings.

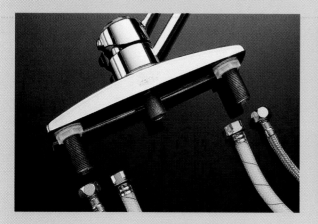

CONNECTING A FAUCET WITH PREATTACHED SUPPLY TUBING

A. *Attach faucet to sink by placing rubber gasket, retainer ring, and locknut onto threaded tailpiece. Tighten locknut with a basin wrench or channel-type pliers. Some center-mounted faucets have a decorative coverplate (inset). Secure coverplate from underneath with washers and locknuts screwed onto coverplate bolts.*

B. *Connect preattached supply tubing to shutoff valves with compression fittings. Red-coded tube should be attached to the hot water pipe, blue-coded to the cold water pipe.*

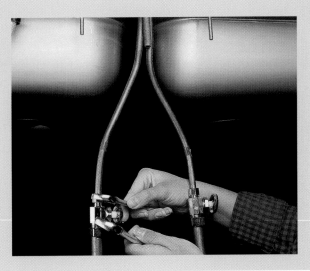

INSTALLING A SINK SPRAYER

A. *Apply a ¼" bead of plumber's putty or silicone caulk to the bottom edge of the sprayer base, and insert the tailpiece of the sprayer base into the sink opening.*

B. *Place a friction washer over the tailpiece. Screw the mounting nut onto the tailpiece and tighten with a basin wrench or channel-type pliers. Wipe away excess putty around the base.*

C. *Screw the sprayer hose onto the hose nipple on the bottom of the faucet. Tighten ¼ turn, using a basin wrench or channel-type pliers.*

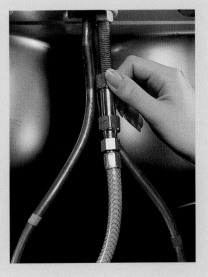

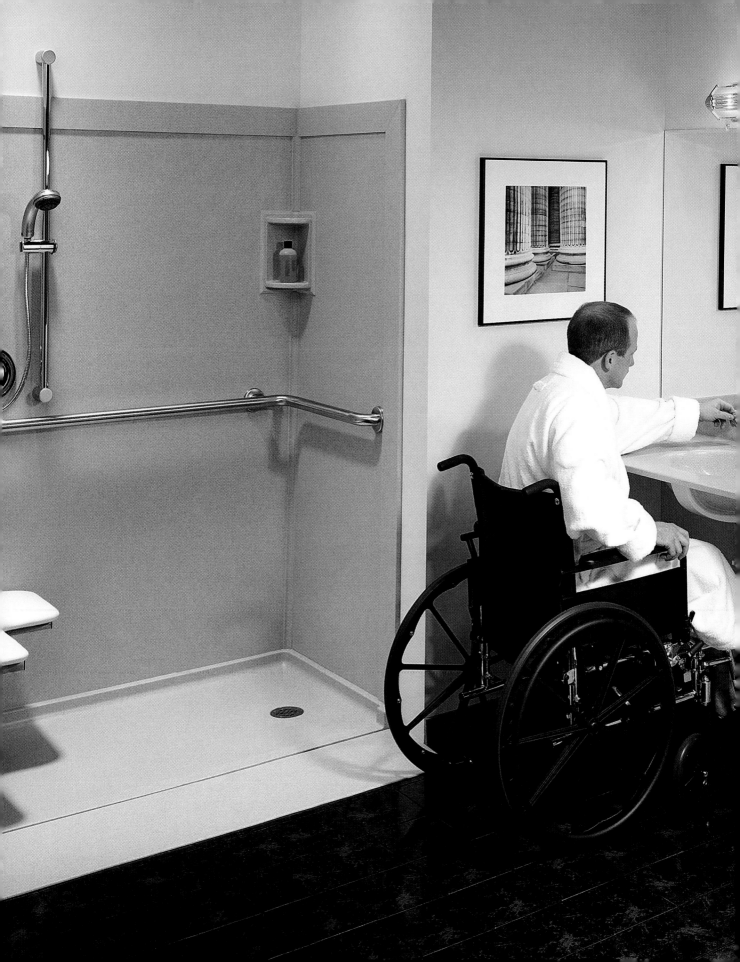

BATHROOMS

The bathroom signifies personal independence more than any other room in the house, but bathroom fixtures and surfaces can present unique obstacles to accessibility.

Through the use of innovative products and accessible design, it's possible to preserve personal independence and promote safety for every member of your family. For example, adding grab bars near showers and tubs can help family members steady themselves on wet, slippery surfaces. Installing a vent fan and heating lamp can help control moisture and make the room warmer for elderly or disabled family members, who may take longer to bathe. And adding a slide-bar showerhead can make bathing more comfortable for standing and sitting bathers, alike.

Whether you're ready to make small changes or completely remodel your bathroom, the pages that follow will offer helpful hints on fixture styles, placement, and features, as well as cabinetry, lighting, and flooring.

Flooring

Make sure bathroom flooring is level and nonslip.

Brush a slip-resistant glaze on new or existing ceramic tile to improve traction, and apply nonslip adhesive strips or decals to tub and shower surfaces. If your bathroom has area rugs, make sure they have rubber backing to prevent slips and falls for people with mobility or vision problems.

When replacing bathroom flooring, choose matte-surface mosaic tiles, vinyl, and cork materials that are nonslip and glare free.

■ **Wheelchair & Walker Modifications:**

• Remove all area rugs so wheels roll smoothly.

Toilet

A standard toilet can be too low for people with limited leg or joint strength. Toilets that are 19" or higher are cumbersome for short people and wheelchair users.

Make toilet height more comfortable by installing a height adapter. These simple products snap onto a toilet to raise the seat

2 to 5". Some models feature grab bars for extra support.

■ **Wheelchair & Walker Modifications:**

• Add a raised seat adapter in an elongated style to make the toilet seat 17 to 18" high and to gain surface area for transfer.

• Install grab bars (page 72) on walls around the toilet for safe transfer to and from the toilet.

• Consider a wall-hung toilet that can be installed at any height and provides more clear space for approach and transfer.

• If transfer to or from the toilet is particularly difficult, consider an adjustable-height toilet or a model with a power-lift seat.

• Install a bidet or an integrated personal hygiene system to help maintain independence.

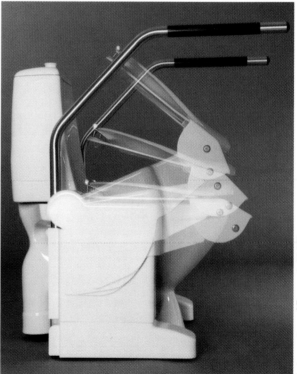

Power-lift toilets benefit people with limited leg or joint strength (above).

Install a toilet with an integrated personal hygiene system (left) to help maintain independence.

A bathroom should be designed with enough approach space and clearance room to allow a wheelchair or walker user to enter and turn around easily. The guidelines for approach spaces (patterned areas) and clearances shown here include ADA guidelines and recommendations from universal design specialists.

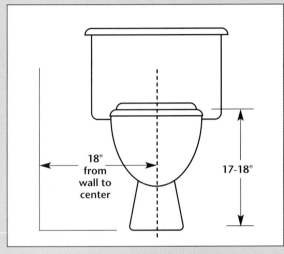

Toilet

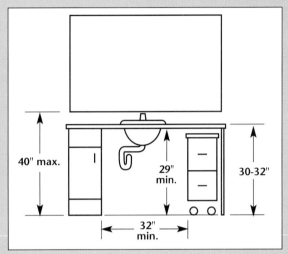

Sink & Vanity

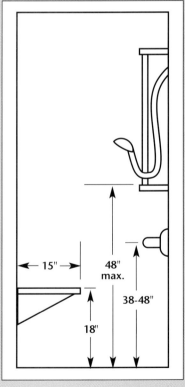

Shower

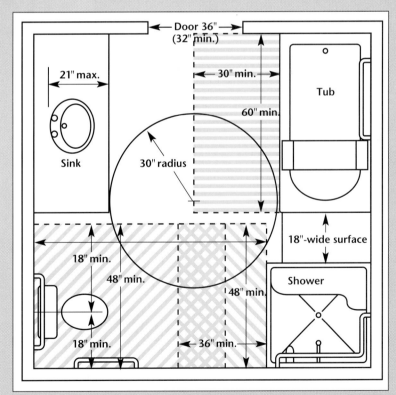

Floor Plan

Sinks & Vanities

Protect people with slow reflexes and limited nerve sensation from burns caused by sudden surges in water temperature by installing scald-guard and volume-control devices on all bathroom faucets.

Consider replacing double-handled faucets with single-lever styles (page 54) that operate with a push, or install motion-sensor faucets for people with limited arm or hand strength. Some faucet styles include a pull-out sprayer, which can be useful to elderly or disabled family members who want to wash their hair without getting in the tub or shower.

Use contrasting colors on countertop edges, grab bars, and towel racks to help people with vision problems mark boundaries.

For people with limited hand strength or mobility, replace vanity drawer and cabinet knobs with C-shaped pull handles, or install magnetic touch latches that require a simple push to operate. Add pull-down hardware to wall-mounted cabinets and medicine cabinets to bring items within reach, or reposition cabinets to minimize reaching.

■ **Wheelchair Modifications:**

• Mount sections of countertop at 34 to 36" for standing users, and 30 to 32" for seated users.

• Provide clear space that is 29" high by 32 to 36" wide under sinks and lowered sections of countertop. Use fold-away doors, remove face frames on base cabinets, or install roll-out base cabinets to gain clear space.

• For a finished look and for level wheelchair access, continue flooring under fold-away or roll-out cabinets. Then insulate pipes or install a protective panel to prevent burns from hot pipes.

• When replacing a sink, choose a style that is shallower at the front and deeper at the drain.

Roll-out base cabinets provide the option of seating space under the counter.

Install a tilted mirror over the vanity so short people and wheelchair users can see into it easily.

Or install a wall-mounted sink, positioned at 30 to 32". Make sure the sink's drain control is accessible and easy to use. A rubber plug with chain is a simple solution.

• Position the sink within 21" of the front of the vanity to minimize reaching. When that's not possible, mount the faucet controls at the side of the sink, rather than the back.

Electrical

Install glare-free, full-spectrum lightbulbs above the vanity to produce truer light for the elderly or people with vision problems. A waterproof light positioned over stand-alone tubs and showers will eliminate shadows and enhance bathing safety. A phone jack and telephone installed near the tub or shower allows family members to call for help if they fall or are injured.

Remove heavy window panels that block natural light, and pull up shades during the day to eliminate shadows. Use motion-sensor or light-sensor nightlights to make nighttime

bathroom visits safer, especially for people with limited mobility or vision problems.

Add an efficient vent fan to reduce moisture and eliminate slippery floors, and choose a vent fan/heating light unit (page 68) to make the bathroom warmer for people sensitive to temperature changes.

Replace all standard outlets (page 66) with ground-fault circuit-interrupters (GFCIs) to protect people with slow reflexes or limited hand strength from sudden electrical shock.

■ **Wheelchair Modifications:**

• Install outlets at a minimum height of 18", and mount countertop receptacles no more than 21" from the front edge of the countertop. A fold-down electrical strip on the sink cabinet can also put outlets within reach.

• Replace standard lights with voice-activated or motion-sensor light fixtures.

• Add a vent fan or automated window opener to keep humidity at bay and reduce slippery surfaces.

Showers & Tubs

Install grab bars (page 72) in and around the shower and tub to provide stability on slippery surfaces.

To make bathing safer and more comfortable for elderly or disabled family members, purchase ready-to-use tub and shower seats from hospital supply stores. Models include transfer seats, seats with backs, and simple stools. Units can be left in the bathroom, or moved out of the way when not in use. If you decide to mount a seat in your tub or shower, install it 18" high, and be sure the seat is at least 15" deep.

Change a standard showerhead to an adjustable showerhead mounted on a vertical slide-bar (page 76) so seated bathers can set the spray at a comfortable height. Some models offer a handheld option that provides even more flexibility.

When remodeling your bathroom, consider a side-access door bathtub that permits easy entry into the tub. A nonslip, soft-sided tub is another option.

For added safety and convenience, reposition water controls and faucets toward the outside edge of the bathtub, at a height of 38 to 48", so people with slow reflexes or limited nerve sensation can adjust the water temperature before getting in to bathe.

■ **Wheelchair Modifications:**

• Install a stand-alone shower with a gently sloping drain base, a pull-down seat, and an adjustable, handheld showerhead. Shower stalls designed to be used without a door or curtain offer the best access. When a curtain is used, install it on a rod mounted securely into wall backing so it can support someone in the event of a fall.

Innovative tub and shower designs make bathing easier for people with disabilities.

Doors

Reverse the bathroom door hinges—including those on showers—so doors open out and family members can be helped if they fall. Consider replacing standard hinges with swing-clear hinges to gain door clearance space.

■ **Wheelchair & Walker Modifications:**

• Widen doorways to 32 to 36" so wheelchair and walker users can enter the bathroom easily (page 20). Or replace a standard door with a pocket door to gain clear space (page 26).

Consider installing a pocket door in your bathroom to gain more clearance room for wheelchairs and walkers.

Photo courtesy of L.E. Johnson Products.

GFCI RECEPTACLE

Ground-fault circuit-interrupters (GFCIs) protect family members with slow reflexes or limited nerve sensation from electrical shock caused by faulty appliances, worn cords or plugs, or accidental water contact with appliances. Because power can be reset at the receptacle, GFCIs also eliminate a trip to the breaker box for the elderly and people with limited mobility.

Because the body of a GFCI receptacle is larger than a standard receptacle, small

crowded electrical boxes may have to be replaced with more spacious boxes.

This project shows you how to install a single-location GFCI receptacle. GFCI receptacles also can be wired to protect all receptacles, switches, and light fixtures from the GFCI "forward" to the end of the circuit (multiple locations).

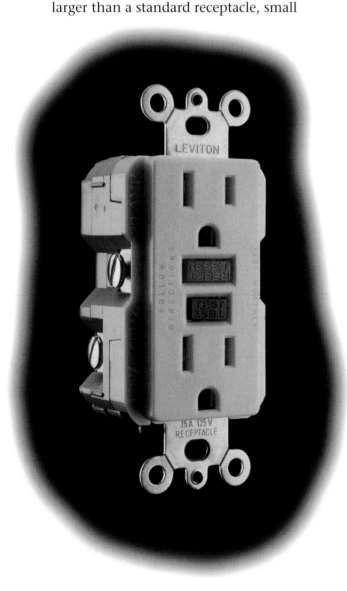

TOOLS & MATERIALS

- Neon circuit tester
- Screwdriver
- Single-location GFCI receptacle
- Wire connectors

HOW TO INSTALL A GFCI RECEPTACLE FOR SINGLE-LOCATION PROTECTION
STEP A: *Removing the Old Receptacle*
1. Shut off power to the receptacle at the main service panel.
2. Test for power with a neon circuit tester by placing one probe of the tester into each slot of the receptacle. Be sure to test both halves of the receptacle. If the circuit tester does not glow, there is no power to the receptacle.
3. Remove the coverplate and the screws securing the receptacle to the electrical box. Without touching the wires, gently pull the receptacle from the box. Test again for power, touching one probe of the circuit tester to a silver screw terminal, and the other probe to a brass screw terminal.
4. Disconnect the wires from the old receptacle.
STEP B: *Installing the GFCI Receptacle*
1. Use a short length of insulated wire to pigtail the white neutral wires together (page 46), and connect the pigtail to the terminal marked WHITE LINE on the GFCI.
2. Pigtail the black hot wires together, and connect them to the terminal marked HOT LINE on the GFCI.
3. If a grounding wire is available, connect it to the green grounding screw terminal of the GFCI. If there is no circuit grounding wire, use a grounding jumper to connect the GFCI grounding screw to the metal box.
4. Carefully tuck all wires back into the receptacle box. Mount the GFCI in the box and reattach the coverplate. Restore power and test the GFCI according to the manufacturer's instructions.

A. *Test the receptacle for power (inset). Then disconnect the wires from the old receptacle.*

B. *Pigtail and connect the black hot wires to the GFCI HOT LINE screw terminals.*

OPTIONS FOR GFCI WIRING

A GFCI wired for single-location protection (shown from the back) has hot and neutral wires connected only to the screw terminals marked LINE. A GFCI connected for single-location protection may be wired as either an end-of-run or middle-of-run configuration.

A GFCI wired for multiple-location protection (shown from the back) has one set of hot and neutral wires connected to the LINE pair of screw terminals and the other set connected to the LOAD pair of screw terminals. A GFCI receptacle connected for multiple-location protection may be wired only as a middle-of-run configuration.

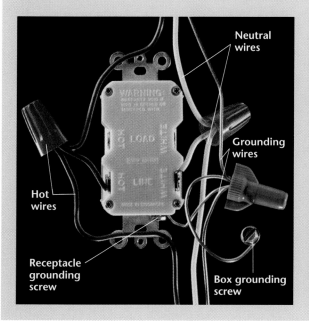

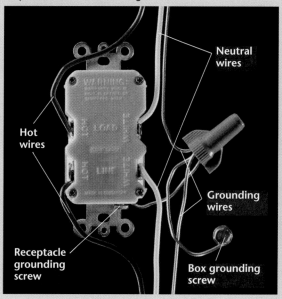

VENT FAN WITH HEATING LAMP

Vent fans with heating lamps reduce moisture in the bathroom and eliminate slippery surfaces for the elderly and people with mobility problems. These units also warm the bathroom, providing a comfortable environment for those sensitive to temperature changes.

Choose a fan that exchanges air at a rate of 8 air changes per hour to prevent the build-up of moisture that can lead to mold and mildew problems. Do not install a vent fan or light directly over a tub or shower, unless it is rated for those areas.

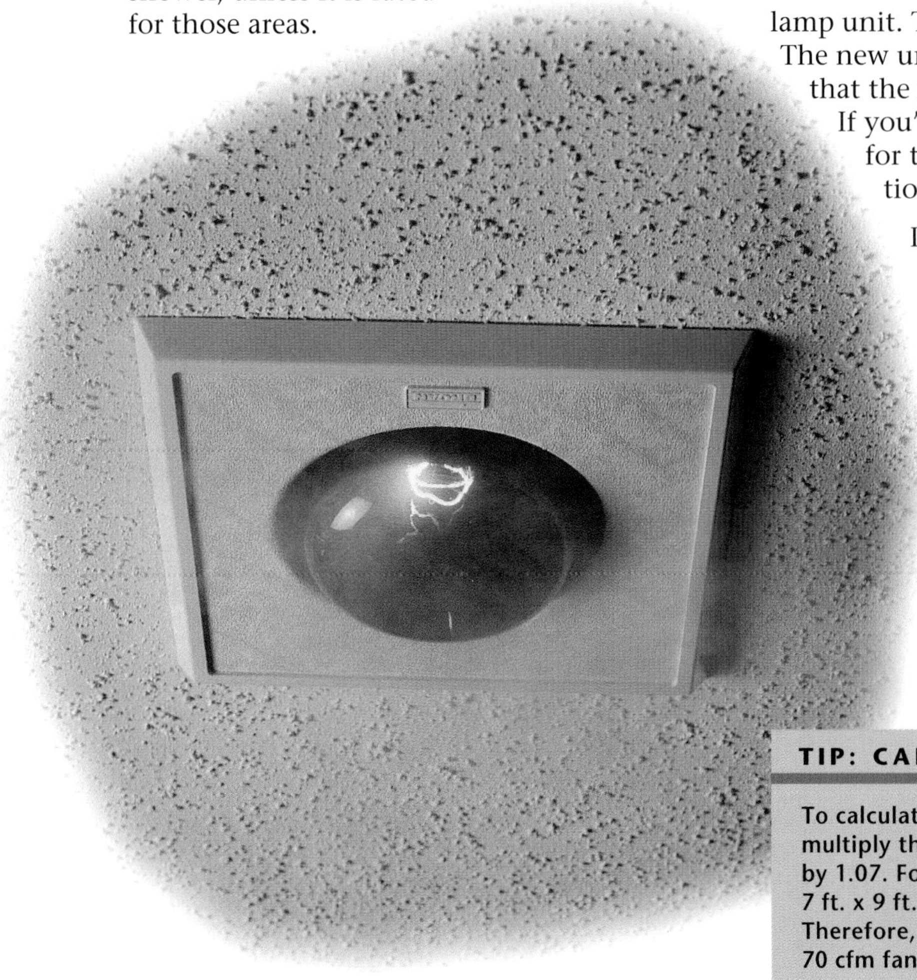

Be aware that sound ratings generally increase with a fan's size and air flow rating (measured in cubic feet per minute, or cfm). Vents rated 1 sone or less are the quietest.

Newer vent fans and heating lights feature ultra-quiet operation and decorative touches, like frosted glass and real wood trim. They blend with bathroom decor, rather than standing out as utility items.

Enhanced-operation features include built-in humidity and motion sensors that automatically switch fans on and off to ensure adequate ventilation. Some models are equipped with automatic nightlights, which can enhance safety for people with limited vision.

The project shown here involves replacing a standard vent fan with a new fan and heating lamp unit. The vent ducting is already in place. The new unit is wired to an existing switch so that the fan and light are operated together. If you'd prefer to have separate controls for the fan and lamp, follow the variation on page 71.

If you are installing a new vent fan, rather than replacing an older model, route the vent through the roof—not into your attic or basement, which can lead to serious moisture damage.

Make sure the fan you choose includes a mounting kit. Many models require a separate purchase for the vent hose (duct), vent tailpiece, and exterior vent cover.

> **TIP: CALCULATING CFM**
>
> To calculate the cfm needed for your bathroom, multiply the room's square footage (floor area) by 1.07. For example, if your bathroom measures 7 ft. x 9 ft., multiply 63 by 1.07 to get 67.4. Therefore, your bathroom would require a 70 cfm fan.

If you do not have attic access above the bathroom, you will need to remove a small portion of the bathroom ceiling to access the existing fan unit. You will also need to connect the vent hose to the new fan unit before installing the unit.

HOW TO INSTALL A VENT FAN WITH HEATING LAMP UNIT

STEP A: *Disconnect & Remove the Old Fan*

1. At the main service panel, turn off the power to the circuit that services the vent fan. Check the fan and switch to make sure the power is off, using the circuit tester.

2. In the bathroom, remove the grill from the old fan, and remove the coverplate to the wiring box inside the fan unit.

3. Disconnect the wires inside the wiring box, then pull the plug connected to the fan motor.

4. Remove the locknut securing the cable clamp to the fan housing.

5. In the attic, pull the cable from the fan housing. Unwrap any insulation from the fan-end of the vent hose, and loosen the hose clamp on the outlet of the fan unit. Remove the hose from the fan.

6. Remove the screws and mounting brackets securing the fan to the ceiling framing, then pull fan from the ceiling opening.

STEP B: *Prepare & Install the New Fan Unit*

1. Slide the adjustable mounting brackets onto the housing of the new vent fan.

2. In the attic, position the fan unit between two joists and extend the mounting brackets. If necessary, enlarge the hole in the ceiling surface to accommodate the new fan. Position the unit so the brackets are flush with the bottoms of the joists and the bottom edge of the housing is flush with the finished ceiling surface (consult the manufacturer's instructions to adjust the brackets for various ceiling thicknesses).

3. Fasten the bracket ends to the joists with 1½" drywall screws.

A. Undo the wire connections on the old vent fan, disconnect the vent ducting, then remove the fan unit.

B. Install the new fan unit in the attic by fastening the mounting brackets to the ceiling joists.

STEP C: *Connect the Vent Hose*

1. Fit the duct connector onto the fan housing, locking it into place. Make sure the damper flap inside the duct connector opens and closes smoothly and that gravity keeps it closed.

2. Attach the vent hose to the duct connector and secure it with the cable clamp. Seal all duct joints with foil duct tape.

3. Wrap the hose with pipe insulation to prevent condensation from forming and dripping into the fan.

STEP D: *Connect the Wiring*

1. Remove the wiring box from the side of the fan housing, then pop out one of the knockouts on the wiring box.

2. If necessary, attach a cable clamp to the circuit cable. Thread the circuit cable wires through the knockout and secure the cable clamp to the wiring box.

3. To wire the unit so that the fan and heating lamp are operated together, join the black (hot) circuit wire to the blue and red wires on the fan, using a wire connector. Join the white (neutral) circuit wire to the white fan wire, then join the green (ground) circuit wire to the grounding lead attached to the wiring box. NOTE: Be sure to check the manufacturer's wiring diagram for specific instructions.

4. Carefully tuck the wires into the wiring box and reattach the box to the fan housing.

5. Insulate around the fan housing, as directed by the manufacturer (some fan types must have an air space between the unit and insulation).

STEP E: *Complete the Installation*

1. If necessary, patch or repair the ceiling surface around the new fan, making sure to seal the front of the fan housing to keep out construction dust.

2. Attach the fan grill to the housing, using the springs provided.

3. Install a BR40 or R40 250W infrared bulb into the bulb socket, and center the grill around the bulb.

4. Turn on the power at the main service panel and test the fan unit.

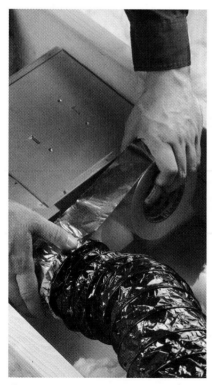

C. *Attach the vent hose, and secure the joints with foil duct tape.*

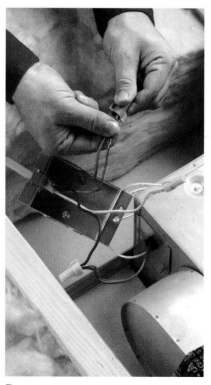

D. *Remove the wiring box from the fan and join the wires with wire connectors.*

E. *Install the fan grill and heating bulb, then center the grill around the bulb.*

Dual-control wiring allows you to operate the vent fan and heating lamp separately, using a double switch. This option requires that you replace a double-wire cable with a three-wire cable (running from the switch box to the fan unit). If you are not able to complete this task yourself, hire an electrician.

STEP A: *Install the New Fan Unit & Three-wire Cable*

1. Follow step A through step C, on pages 69 to 70, to remove the old fan and install the new fan.

2. Remove the coverplate on the switch box. Remove the mounting screws securing the fan switch to the box, and pull the switch out of the box to expose the circuit wires.

3. Disconnect the circuit wires from the switch.

4. Replace the old two-wire circuit cable running from the switch to the fan unit with a three-wire NM cable of the same gauge.

5. Strip the ends of the new cable and secure it to the switch box as it was done with the old cable.

STEP B: *Install the Double Switch*

1. Connect the black (hot) wire from the power source cable to the appropriate screw terminal on the double switch. Join the white (neutral) wire from the source cable to the white wire in the three-wire cable, using a wire connector. Join the ground wires from the two cables to a pigtail connected to the grounding terminal on the double switch.

2. Connect the black (hot) and red (hot) wires from the three-wire cable to separate screw terminals on the switch.

3. Carefully tuck the wires into the box and mount the switch. Install the coverplate.

STEP C: *Wire the Fan Unit & Complete the Installation*

1. Complete step D, on page 70, making the following change to #3: Use wire connectors to join the red (hot) circuit wire to the red unit wire; the black (hot) circuit wire to the blue unit wire; the white (neutral) circuit wire to the white unit wire; and the grounding circuit wire to the grounding lead in the wiring box.

2. Complete step E, on page 70.

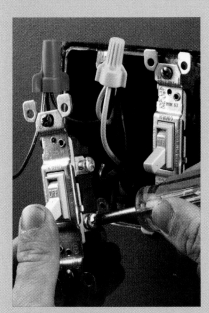

A. *With the power off, remove the old switch and cable, then route the new three-wire cable and secure it to the switch box.*

B. *Connect the source cable and new three-wire cable to the double switch.*

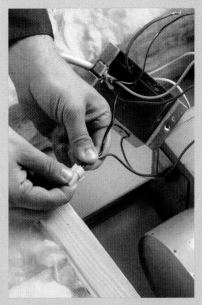

C. *Make the wiring connections at the fan wiring box.*

GRAB BARS

Grab bars help family members steady themselves on slippery shower, tub, and floor surfaces, and they provide support for wheelchair transfers.

A variety of grab bar colors, shapes, sizes, and textures are now available to complement any bathroom decor. To ensure safety throughout the bathroom, install a combination of grab bars near the tub, shower, and toilet, following the recommendations listed on page 73.

Choose a bar style with a 1¼ to 1½" diameter that fits comfortably between your thumb and fingers. Then install grab bars 1½" from the wall with anchors that can support at least 250 pounds.

If you are remodeling your bathroom and will have the wall framing exposed, add blocking or backing for securing grab bars. Use 2 × 6 or 2 × 8 lumber to provide room for ajustments, and fasten the blocks to the framing with 16d nails. Note the locations of your blocking for future reference.

When installing grab bars where no wall supports exist, use specialized, heavy-duty, hollow-wall anchors designed to support at least 250 pounds.

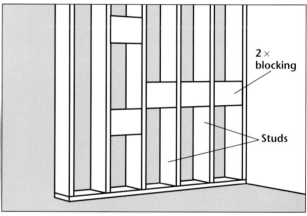

The easiest way to install grab bars is to screw them into wall studs, into blocking, or into backing attached to studs.

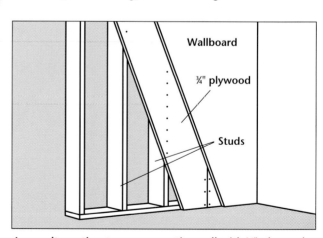

As an alternative, cover your entire wall with ¾" plywood backing secured with screws to your wall framing, so you can install grab bars virtually anywhere on the wall.

Photo courtesy of Ginger®.

These suggestions for grab bar placement include ADA guidelines and recommendations from universal design specialists.

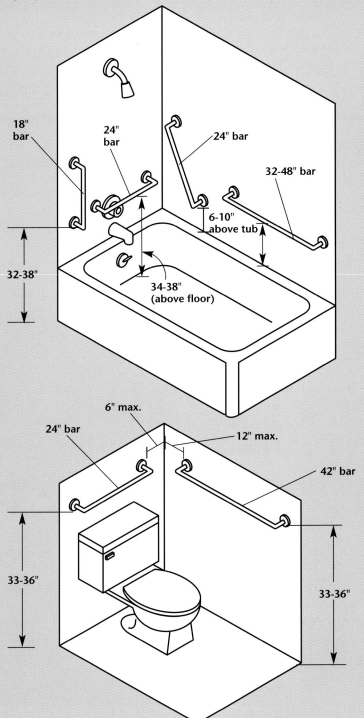

18" bar

24" bar

24" bar

32-48" bar

6-10" above tub

32-38"

34-38" (above floor)

6" max.

24" bar

12" max.

42" bar

33-36"

33-36"

Tub/Shower:

Vertical bar: (18" long) at entrance to tub; bottom of bar 32 to 38" above the floor.

Horizontal bar on control wall: 24" long; 34 to 38" above the floor.

Horizontal bar on back wall: 32 to 48" long; 34 to 38" above the floor for shower only; 6 to 10" above top of tub for bath only.

Angled bar: 24" long; bottom end 6 to 10" above top of tub (not necessary in stand-alone showers).

Toilet:

Horizontal bar at side: 42" long (min.); 12" (max.) from the back wall; 33 to 36" above the floor.

Horizontal bar behind: 24" long (min.); 6" (max.) from the side wall; 33 to 36" above the floor.

TOOLS & MATERIALS

- Measuring tape
- Pencil
- Studfinder
- Level
- Drill & bits
- Grab bar
- Silicone caulk
- #12 stainless steel screws
- Hollow-wall anchors

HOW TO INSTALL GRAB BARS INTO WOOD FRAMING OR BACKING

STEP A: *Locate the Studs & Mark the Bar Location*

1. Locate the wall studs in the installation area, using a studfinder. If the area is tiled, the studfinder may not detect studs, so try to locate the studs above the tile, if possible, then use a level to transfer the marks lower on the wall. Otherwise, drill small, exploratory holes through grout joints in the tile, then fill the holes with silicone caulk to seal them. Be careful not to drill into pipes.

2. Mark the grab bar height at one stud location, then use a level to transfer the height mark to the stud that will receive the other end of the bar.

3. Position the grab bar on the height marks so at least two of the three mounting holes are aligned with the stud centers. Mark the mounting hole locations onto the wall.

4. Drill pilot holes for the mounting screws. If you're drilling through tile, use a masonry bit and put masking tape on the tile to prevent the bit from sliding on the glazed surface. For screws that won't hit studs, drill holes for wall anchors, following the manufacturer's directions for sizing. Install anchors, if necessary (page 75).

STEP B: *Install the Bar*

1. Apply a continuous bead of silicone caulk to the back side of each bar end.

2. Secure the bar to the studs using #12 stainless steel screws (the screws should penetrate the stud by at least 1"). If you're using wall anchors, install a stainless steel screw or bolt into each anchor.

3. Test the bar to make sure it's secure.

A. *Locate the studs with a studfinder (inset). Center the bar ends over studs or backing and mark the mounting screw holes.*

B. *Apply caulk to the bar ends (inset), then fasten the bar to the studs (and anchors) with stainless steel screws.*

Wall anchors are available for a variety of grab bar applications. Make sure the anchors you use can support 250 pounds (contact the grab bar manufacturer for the recommended anchor for your project). Always follow the manufacturer's instructions when installing anchors.

WingIt™ anchors are heavy-duty hollow-wall anchors designed to support grab bars that can't be secured to framing or backing. When installed in walls of ½" wallboard with ceramic tile or in a ¼"-thick fiberglass tub surround, WingIts hold up to 1000 pounds; in ⅝" wallboard alone, 450 pounds; and in ½" wallboard alone, up to 250 pounds. Once installed, the anchor's wing assembly is 3" in diameter, so the bar must be located where no stud interferes.

WingIt anchors are prepared for insertion and temporarily mounted to the grab bar, then are inserted into 1¼" holes. Waterproof adhesive rings hold the anchors in place, and the bar is removed. A tap on the center bolt springs the wing assembly, and the bolt is tightened to draw the wing to the back of the wall. The grab bar is fastened to the anchor mounting plates with stainless steel screws.

TOGGLER® brand SNAPTOGGLE™ anchors help secure grab bars to steel studs. This additional reinforcement is important because bare screws can strip or pull out of light-gauge steel. At each end of the bar, one SNAPTOGGLE is used to secure the top screw of the mounting flange to the stud. For the remaining two screws at each end, one is driven into the stud, if possible, and the other is secured to the wall with a hollow wall anchor.

The end of the anchor is inserted into a ½" hole drilled through the center of the stud. A collar is slid along the straps of the anchor to snug it against the back side of the stud. The straps are then broken off, and a ¼"-20 stainless steel bolt is inserted through the grab bar flange and screwed into the anchor.

The TOGGLER brand SNAPTOGGLE anchor is available in stainless steel and zinc-plated steel. It is important to match the steel of the anchor, bolt, and grab bar—stainless steel is best for damp conditions.

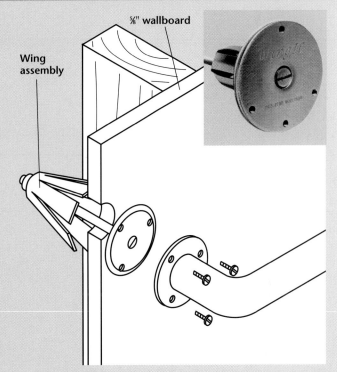

⅝" wallboard

Wing assembly

WingIt™ Anchor

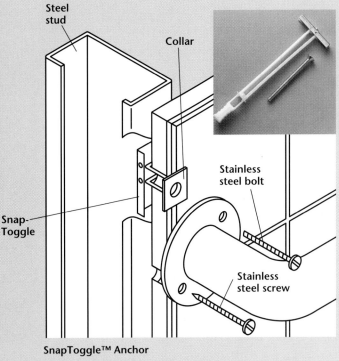

Steel stud

Collar

Snap-Toggle

Stainless steel bolt

Stainless steel screw

SnapToggle™ Anchor

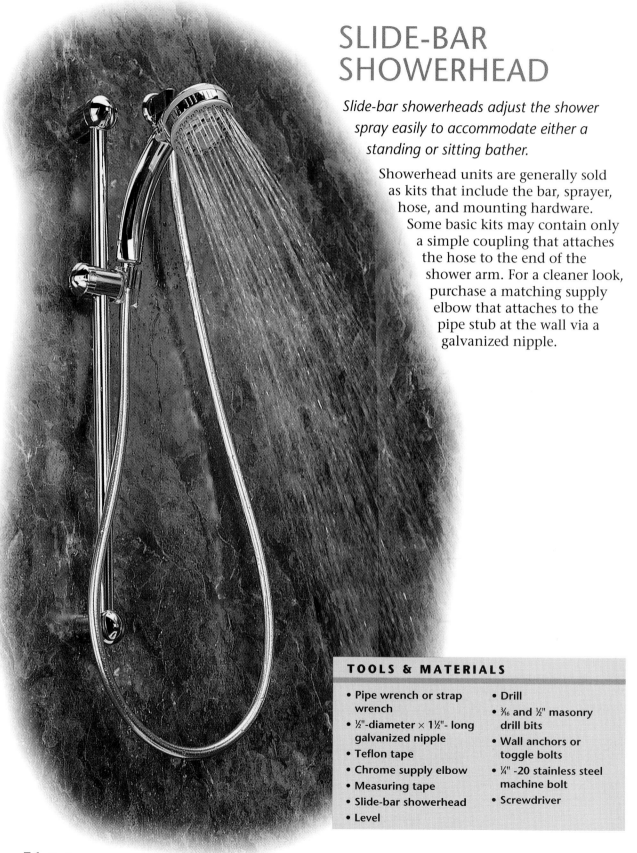

SLIDE-BAR SHOWERHEAD

Slide-bar showerheads adjust the shower spray easily to accommodate either a standing or sitting bather.

Showerhead units are generally sold as kits that include the bar, sprayer, hose, and mounting hardware. Some basic kits may contain only a simple coupling that attaches the hose to the end of the shower arm. For a cleaner look, purchase a matching supply elbow that attaches to the pipe stub at the wall via a galvanized nipple.

TOOLS & MATERIALS

- Pipe wrench or strap wrench
- ½"-diameter × 1½"- long galvanized nipple
- Teflon tape
- Chrome supply elbow
- Measuring tape
- Slide-bar showerhead
- Level
- Drill
- 3⁄16 and ½" masonry drill bits
- Wall anchors or toggle bolts
- ¼" -20 stainless steel machine bolt
- Screwdriver

HOW TO INSTALL A SLIDE-BAR SHOWERHEAD

STEP A: *Remove Showerhead & Attach Supply Elbow*

1. Remove the existing showerhead and arm.

2. Wrap the threads of the galvanized nipple with Teflon tape and thread it into the stub-out. Leave about ½" of the nipple protruding from the wall.

3. Wrap the exposed nipple threads with Teflon tape. Apply a bead of silicone caulk around the inside of the escutcheon (decorative cover). Thread the supply elbow onto the nipple. Cover the elbow with a soft cloth to prevent scratches, and tighten it with a pipe wrench or strap wrench.

STEP B: *Mount the Slide-Bar*

1. Attach a mounting bracket to each end of the slide-bar.

2. Place the bar 4 to 6" to the side of the wall supply elbow to avoid the water pipes. Locate the lower end of the bar about 48" from the bottom of the tub or shower. Use a level to make sure the bar is plumb, then mark the location of the mounting holes.

3. Drill holes in the tile using a ³⁄₁₆" masonry bit. If you hit a stud, attach the slide-bar to the wall using the screws and wall anchors provided with the kit. If you do not hit a stud, use a toggle anchor rated to 250 pounds (page 75). Apply silicone caulk under the slide-bar mounts before tightening.

STEP C: *Finish Unit Assembly*

1. Slide the decorative end caps onto the mounting brackets.

2. Thread the shower hose onto the supply elbow.

3. Slip the showerhead into the slide-lock mechanism.

A. *Attach the supply elbow to the galvanized nipple.*

B. *Position the bar, and mark mounting holes. Attach bar to the wall with the screws and the anchors provided (inset).*

C. *Thread the showerhose onto the supply elbow, and clip the showerhead into the slide-lock mechanism.*

BEDROOMS

Whether it's shared or private, a guest room or a personal retreat, a bedroom is a sanctuary where body and spirit are renewed.

Rethink, redesign, and redecorate the bedroom so every family member can maintain true personal space for sleeping, relaxing, and recuperating. Take advantage of an adjustable closet system and the hundreds of innovative accessories that put clothes at a comfortable height. Use technology to turn off lights and control heating and cooling by remote control or preset selection. And install "smart house" products to close windows and answer the front door.

If you're designing a guest suite to accommodate family members' special needs, you'll find dozens of ideas for creating a safe and comfortable home away from home.

Photo courtesy of IKEA.

Flooring

Choose dense, low-pile bedroom flooring materials, such as berber carpeting or cork, to help the elderly or people with mobility problems maintain their footing. Add a contrasting border around the room's edge to help people with vision problems mark room boundaries.

Look for nonslip, matte surface finishes in wood, ceramic tile, or sheet vinyl to reduce glare.

■ **Wheelchair & Walker Modifications:**

• Choose dense, low-pile flooring, such as berber carpet, cork, wood, or ceramic tile, so wheels can roll smoothly. Select matte finishes to prevent slipping.

Room Arrangement

Design the bedroom with plenty of open floor space from the bed to the nearest bathroom. Use hanging storage to hold hobby materials, books, bags, shoes, and accessories.

Position bedside tables, chairs, and lamps so they won't interfere with getting into or out of bed for people with limited vision or mobility problems.

■ **Wheelchair & Walker Modifications:**

• Align dressers and other large furniture against the wall to create clear floor space.

Lighting & Electrical

Use a combination of natural and artificial light to reduce glare and shadows for people with vision problems.

Full-spectrum, high-intensity lightbulbs provide better light for people with limited vision,

A closet organizer system puts clothes at a comfortable height for both disabled and able-bodied family members.

and three-way bulbs offer adjustability for people who are sensitive to light.

Add lights where necessary, such as near a chair or on a bedside table. Add electrical outlets where needed, and keep cords safely out of walking paths. When wiring is not practical, hang touch lights on the wall.

Look for easy-to-use lamp features, such as long pull chains and large switches, or consider a device that turns lights on with a touch when hand strength is an issue.

Use automatic plug-in nightlights to illuminate pathways to the kitchen or bathroom. Motion-sensor room lights that turn on and off automatically when someone enters the room are especially beneficial to people with limited mobility, vision, hand strength, or memory. Consider installing them in closets, as well.

Keep a telephone in the bedroom so disabled family members can call for help in case of an emergency. Choose large-button, lighted key-pads for people with limited vision or hand strength.

■ **Wheelchair & Walker Modifications:**

• Mount electrical outlets 18 to 30" above the floor to reduce bending and reaching.

• Install automated window coverings, lighting, and heating controls.

Beds

If getting into and out of bed is difficult, add a handrail to the bed. Most styles are adjustable and attach to the bed frame without tools.

Consider an electric bed if you or a family member suffers from a medical condition such as circulatory problems or breathing disorders. Electric sleep systems allow you to raise the bottom or the top portions of the mattress independently for maximum comfort.

Choose a mattress that supports your sleep style and age, and look for a bed frame that allows your feet to touch the floor when you're seated on the bed. If the frame is too tall, cut it down or purchase a shorter base. Bed frames are available in heights from 3 to 7". Boxsprings also come in a variety of thicknesses.

■ **Wheelchair Modifications:**

• Choose a bed frame that aligns the mattress height with the wheelchair seat height for easier transfer.

Furniture

When space permits, include a chair in the bedroom for reading and talking on the phone. Firm furniture styles make rising easier for the elderly or people with mobility problems.

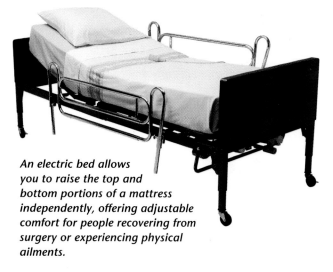

An electric bed allows you to raise the top and bottom portions of a mattress independently, offering adjustable comfort for people recovering from surgery or experiencing physical ailments.

When limited leg or joint strength is an issue, consider chairs with automated risers that lift and tilt the seat.

Repair sticky drawers and rollers on dressers and closets. For people with limited hand strength, replace drawer knobs with C-shaped handles or magnetic latches that can be opened with a simple push or pull.

Closets

Install an adjustable closet system (page 84) to put items within reach.

Choose a system that will support the weight of your items. Wire systems are a quick, low-cost solution to closet organizing, but they can bend and sag over time. Wood is sturdier and provides shelf storage for heavy items.

Consider a wall-hung system instead of a floor-anchored organizer to provide roll-under access for wheelchairs and to make vacuuming and floor-covering replacement easier in the future.

Look for adjustable rods and add-on features, such as tie racks, fold-down pants racks, and pull-out baskets, to customize your closet system.

If room permits, add a separate dressing area in the bathroom so elderly people can retain body heat by dressing immediately after bathing.

■ **Wheelchair & Walker Modifications:**

• Provide 5 ft. of clear floor space for closet access.

• Install a carousel closet system to bring clothes to the door of small closets.

Include a seating area in the bathroom (above), so family members can rest while getting ready.

Take advantage of closet accessories like shoe and tie racks (left) to put clothing items within reach.

A guest suite is different from a guest room. A suite is often a home away from home for a recuperating relative or aging parent.

Because they are intended for long-term visits, guest suites offer more of the conveniences of home. Your guest suite might include a sleeping room, laundry facility, kitchenette, and bathroom.

Locate the guest suite away from the confusion of family life, but in a convenient part of the house. It's important to provide comfort, safety, and privacy for guests, as well as convenient access to family members and entrances. Consider a separate walk-out entrance, stairlift, or elevator, depending on your needs.

If you're planning a suite for an elderly or physically disabled family member, safety and usability should guide your design. Some safety features are required by local building codes, such as an egress window or door for emergency exit in case of fire. Other elements will be dictated by your residents' needs. You might consider installing an intercom system in the guest suite for communication between the suite and the main house.

©Robert Perron

Photo courtesy of U-Line.

Including a kitchen in your suite can be a great convenience. A popular option is the morning kitchen—a small area with a coffee-maker, small sink, instant hot-water dispenser, and under-cabinet refrigerator. Larger kitchens might include a toaster, microwave, small dishwasher, cooktop, and oven.

Plan at least one section of lowered countertop with under-cabinet knee space, and install shelving and appliances that can be reached by a seated user. Even if your family doesn't need these features today, including them in your design will give you greater flexibility in the future.

If space permits, include a full-sized bathroom as part of your guest suite. Remember that people of all sizes and abilities may use your guest bath, so design it to be as accessible as possible. Include safety features such as anti-scald devices on faucets and grab bars or blocking for bars in showers.

ADJUSTABLE CLOSET SYSTEM

An adjustable closet system puts clothes and accessories within reach for people of all sizes and abilities.

Build your own closet system to attain accessibility features like roll-under space, as well as adjustable shelves and rods. Add closet accessories, such as hooks, additional rods or shelves, pull-out drawers, baskets, slide-out belt and shoe racks, and fold-down pants racks to customize your system.

The closet organizer shown here can be adapted to fit almost any closet. It has a simple plywood cabinet with three adjustable shelves and space above and below for additional storage and easy access.

Use finish-grade plywood for the cabinet and support piece. Then paint, stain, or protect the wood with a clear finish. Solid wood trim covers the plywood edges and lends strength to the shelves. For this, you can use clear pine, which has few knots, or a hardwood, such as aspen, oak, or maple.

The shelves shown in this project are 11" deep. You may want to make them deeper. Just keep in mind that shelves longer than 36" may require additional support to prevent sagging.

HOW TO BUILD THE CLOSET SYSTEM
STEP A: *Cut the Plywood Pieces*
1. From a 4 × 8-ft. sheet of ¾" plywood, cut the two cabinet sides, the side support, and the cabinet top and bottom. Use a table saw or a circular saw with a straightedge guide, and measure carefully so the

TOOLS & MATERIALS

- Measuring tape
- Circular saw
- Straightedge cutting guide
- Drill
- Router w/straight bit
- Hacksaw
- Framing square
- Nail set
- Studfinder
- Level
- ¾" × 4 × 8 ft. finish-grade plywood
- ¾" × 4 × 4 ft. finish-grade plywood
- ½" × 4 × 8 ft. finish-grade plywood
- (2) 10-ft.-long 1 × 2 trim
- (1) 8-ft.-long 1 × 2 trim
- (1) 8-ft.-long 1 × 1 trim
- ⅝" screws
- 2½" trim-head screws
- 2" coarse-thread drywall screws
- 6d finish nails
- Wood glue
- Wood finishing materials
- 1¼"-dia. × 6 ft. closet rod
- Metal shelf standards w/shelf clips & closet rod hangers

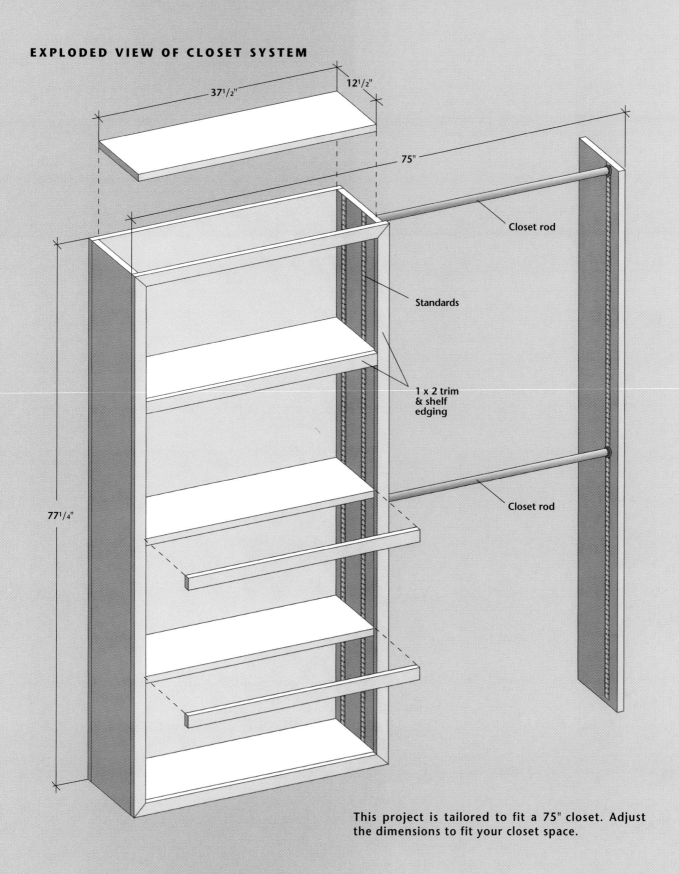

37¹/₂"

12¹/₂"

75"

Closet rod

Standards

1 x 2 trim
& shelf
edging

Closet rod

77¹/₄"

This project is tailored to fit a 75" closet. Adjust
the dimensions to fit your closet space.

cuts are straight and the pieces uniform. The saw will remove ⅛" of material with each cut, so the sheet can be ripped into four 11⅞"-wide pieces. Cut the cabinet sides and side support at 11⅞ × 77¼", and cut the cabinet top and bottom at 11⅞ × 36".

2. From a 4 × 4-ft. sheet of ¾" plywood, cut the three shelves at 11⅞ × 35⅞".

3. Cut the cabinet back at 37½ × 77¼", using a 4 × 8-ft. sheet of ½" plywood.

STEP B: *Install the Shelf Standards*

1. Mark the locations of the grooves that will receive the metal shelf standards for the cabinet shelves. On the inside faces of the cabinet sides, make a mark 1" from the side edges. These marks represent the outside edges of the standards. You can make these standards as long as you wish: they can run the full length of the sides or stop short of the ends.

2. Mark the grooves for the closet rod standards on the outside face of the right cabinet side piece and the inside face of the side support. Make marks for one standard on each piece, 2" from the front edge. If you want the option of installing shelves on this side of the system, you can install an additional

standard on each piece, 2" from the rear edge.

3. Using a router fitted with a straight bit that matches the width of the standards, cut the groove, using a straightedge guide to ensure straight cuts. The depth of the grooves should match the thickness of the standards.

4. Cut the standards to length as needed, using a hacksaw. Set the cabinet sides together with their ends aligned. Lay the standards into the grooves and use a framing square to make sure all the standard slots are aligned so the shelves will be level. Fasten the standards to the sides with the included nails or ⅝" screws.

STEP C: *Assemble the Cabinet*

1. Using wood glue and 2½" trim-head screws, fasten the cabinet top and bottom pieces between the ends of the cabinet sides. Make sure the outside faces of the top and bottom are flush with the ends of the sides.

2. Before the glue dries, fasten the back panel to the cabinet, using 2" coarse-thread drywall screws driven every 12". As you work, make sure the cabinet is flush with the edges of the back panel—this will keep the cabinet square. Let the glue dry.

A. *Cut the plywood pieces using a straightedge cutting guide.*

B. *Rout the dado grooves. Then use a framing square (inset) to align the shelf standards.*

C. *Assemble the cabinet sides, top, and bottom, then add the plywood back.*

STEP D: *Add the Trim*

1. Cut the 1 × 2 trim to fit around the cabinet, using 45° miter joints at the corners. Test-fit the pieces as you work. Position the top edge of the upper horizontal trim piece flush with the top of the cabinet. Position the top edge of the lower horizontal trim flush with the top of the cabinet bottom. Position the outside edges of the side trim flush with the cabinet sides. Fasten the trim to the front cabinet edges with wood glue and 6d finish nails. If necessary, drill pilot holes for the nails to prevent the trim from splitting. Use a nail set to drive the nail heads slightly below the surface.

2. Cut the 1 × 1 trim piece at 77¼" and fasten it to the front edge of the side support with glue and finish nails. Make sure the outside edge of the trim is flush with the outside face of the side support.

3. Cut the 1 × 2 shelf trim at 34⅜". Fasten each piece to the front edge of a shelf so the ends of the trim are ¾" from the shelf ends and the top edges are flush.

4. If desired, sand and finish wood pieces.

STEP E: *Install the Cabinet & Shelves*

1. Use a studfinder (page 74) to locate and mark the wall studs in the areas where you'll install the cabinet and side support. Make light pencil marks at both edges of each stud, marking above the area that will be covered by the cabinet and side support.

2. Position the cabinet in the closet corner, using temporary blocks to prop it up 6" above the floor.

3. Fasten the cabinet in place, driving 2½" trim-head screws through the side and back pieces and into the wall studs. Space the screws about 16" apart.

4. Install the shelves using clips set into the standards.

STEP F: *Install the Side Support & Closet Rods*

1. Measure over and align the top of the cabinet. Then mark the cabinet height onto the opposing closet wall.

2. Position the side support against the wall so its top end is on the height mark and its rear edge is ½" from the back wall. Fasten the support to the wall studs with 2½" trim-head screws.

3. Insert closet rod hangers into the standards on the outside of the cabinet and the side support.

4. Measure between the hangers, cut the rods to fit, and install them.

D. *Install trim along the front edges of the cabinet, shelves, and side support, then use a nail punch to set the nails.*

E. *Mount the cabinet to the closet wall so its bottom edge is 6" above the floor.*

F. *Install the side support at the cabinet height, then cut the closet rods to fit.*

HOME OFFICE &
HOBBY ROOMS

An accident or sudden disability may require you or a family member to temporarily or permanently work at home.

Whether you already have a home office or are considering devoting some space to surfing the Internet and sending E-mail to family and friends, your work space can be comfortable and accessible with some thoughtful consideration given to room design, desk style, software, and accessories. Wiring your home office for the Internet and E-mail will bring information to you and help you stay in touch, no matter where you conduct business.

If you're looking for a way to relax, consider dedicating a space to your favorite hobby or pastime. A sunny room with panoramic views is the perfect place to paint, practice guitar, work on puzzles, or unwind. Built-in shelving and rolling carts help keep hobby supplies out of sight but accessible.

The ideas that follow will help you choose a location, plan your space, consider electrical needs, and select furniture to create a home office or hobby room that meets both your physical and organizational needs.

Home Office Wiring

If you are working at home temporarily, stay in touch with coworkers and friends with a simple Internet and E-mail connection. Computer systems devoted entirely to these functions are available from most computer manufacturers.

If you need word processing or other software to complete work at home, look for a computer system with features that enhance accessibility, such as non-glare, high-resolution screens, full-sized keyboards, and easy-access switches. For maximum versatility, consider wireless models.

Determine your computer usage and your demand for reliability and speed to decide if you need dial-in or cable access service. Shop and compare service providers in your area for prices and packaging.

When your home office space serves as a primary or secondary work space, install a video jack (F-connector) to provide connections for receiving and redistributing TV, VCR, DVD, and closed-circuit camera signals. A universal remote will make using all of your equipment easier.

Your home office wiring also should include at least one voice/data (RJ45) jack for phone and data lines, as well as multi-line computer data connections.

For maximum performance, consider a home network system that brings all the office electrical systems together in one location. A hub—or distribution center—is typically mounted in a basement or a utility closet to receive the phone, Internet, cable or satellite TV lines, as well as stereo and video connections from an entertainment center in the home.

The hub amplifies incoming signals and sends them along high-performance cabling and wire to plug-and-play outlets throughout the house.

Multimedia outlets can be tailored to the specific needs of each room. Outlets contain a series of jacks and connectors for plug-and-play connection.

A distribution hub brings all the modules, cables, and wire connections together in one place. A plastic cover (inset) provides protection and allows easy access to the system.

Be sure to check with your local building department about codes for home network wiring.

■ **Wheelchair Modifications:**
 • Position plug-and-play outlets 18" above the floor.

Locating Your Office or Hobby Room

Locate your office or hobby room away from family areas, to define workspace and maintain privacy. Main floor rooms offer the best accessibility for wheelchairs and people with vision or mobility problems.

If clients or delivery personnel will be regular visitors to your home office, locate it near an entrance on the main floor. This creates a safer and more professional environment because clients won't need to walk through your living areas.

If you are creating a home office for family use, convert an extra room or carve a space from another room in the house. Armoires and other decorative cabinetry can store supplies behind closed doors when not in use. Look for pull-out desktops that provide roll-under access and adequate knee space and drawers that slide out easily and fully.

■ **Wheelchair & Walker Modifications:**

• Locate the office or hobby room on the main floor.

• Consider an elevator when the office or hobby room is located on another level of the house.

• Add a ramp or lift to the house when exterior stairways present an obstacle.

Room Layouts

There are four typical layouts for home offices or hobby rooms. Choose the arrangement that works best for you, based on your desktop and storage needs, available space, and accessibility needs.

Wall layouts are simple, with the desk and storage units aligned along one wall. Although this arrangement is a good choice for rooms with limited space, it is less efficient than other arrangements, because storage units are not always within easy reach for people with back injuries, limited arm strength, or mobility problems.

L-shaped layouts are the most effective for a corner, and they provide roll-up access to a large work surface. You also can use this configuration to divide a space, by placing one leg of the "L" against a wall and letting the other leg project into the room.

Parallel layouts provide two desks or tables set a few feet apart, with a chair between them. This arrangement makes it easy to separate your work by task. For example, you can set your computer on one surface and your files and phone on the other. However, this arrangement doesn't usually provide enough floor space for wheelchair access.

U-shaped layouts create the most effecient work or hobby area, because all of the elements are within easy reach for people with mobility problems. The outside surface of the desk can create a small conference area or roll-up access for wheelchairs.

■ **Wheelchair & Walker Modifications:**

• Choose a wall layout for easy access.

• Position an L-shaped layout in a corner.

• Use the outside edge of a U-shaped layout for wheelchair access.

Lighting

Office and hobby rooms require both task and ambient lighting, especially for seated users and

TIP: ERGONOMICS

To minimize discomfort and fatigue, include ergonomic design in your office plan. Choose chairs and desktops that fit your body type and size.

Your chair should be fully adjustable, so you can set the height, back, seat, and arms exactly where you want them.

Primary work surfaces should be at least 24" wide and stand between 28 and 30" from the floor, with a leg clearance of at least 25". Make sure there's at least 34" of space between your work surface and any opposing walls. You'll need even more if you or another office worker uses a wheelchair or walker.

Position your keyboard slightly lower than your elbows as you type, typically 25 to 29" above the floor. Your monitor should be at or below eye level to avoid eye and neck strain.

people with limited vision. Overall lighting should be even to reduce shadows and glare.

Add a lamp to increase desktop lighting. Models with long chains, easy switches, or touch turn-on devices are best for people with limited hand strength and vision. Floor lamps can improve ambient lighting in rooms with insufficient overhead lighting. Consider automated lighting systems for the elderly and people with limited vision or memory problems.

Compensate for variable outside light with adjustable indoor lighting. Fit fixtures with three-way bulbs or dimmer switches to customize lighting intensity. If you work at a computer, add track lighting that can be directed to eliminate shadows and glare. Long-life bulbs reduce the need for replacement, and are a benefit for people with mobility problems.

Choose fluorescent bulbs for overhead fixtures, and position your desk betweeen lighting

elements to minimize glare. Cover lights with opaque or louvered shades to dim the light for people sensitive to glare or bright light, or install dimmer switches.

If clients visit your home office, your insurance carrier may require outdoor lighting. Use spot and overhead lighting at entrances to aid the elderly or people with mobility problems. Add landscape lighting to brighten walkways, floodlights to light up parking areas, and entryway lights to welcome elderly guests and people with limited vision or mobility (page 120).

■ **Wheelchair & Walker Modifications:**
- Mount track lights on the wall, so fixtures can be adjusted from a seated position.
- Install motion-sensor lights.

Windows
Glare from lighting, windows, keyboards, desktops, and other shiny surfaces can be a problem for the elderly or people with limited vision.

Position your desk or work counter at a right angle to the window, rather than facing or opposing it, to reduce reflections and to cut down on glare off your desktop.

Choose the desk layout that will work best for you and the work you perform most often in your office or hobby room. Wall- and L-shaped layouts (left) offer wheelchair access, while parallel- or U-shaped layouts (above) offer additional desk space.

Reduce reflections with anti-glare window films and full-length adjustable curtains, blinds, or shades—which also help absorb background noise for people with hearing difficulties. Add an anti-glare panel or screen to your computer monitor to ease eyestrain.

Automated window openers and window covering openers allow the elderly or people with limited arm or hand strength to easily adjust lighting, privacy, and ventilation.

■ **Wheelchair & Walker Modifications:**

- Install automated window coverings.
- Keep pathways to windows clear.
- Lower windows, so a seated person can see outside, and install sill-level latches.
- Consider automated window openers.

Desks

Choose a desk that fits your home office or hobby room activity. Consider how much equipment you have and where you want it located. If you want your printer or pottery wheel on the desktop, you'll need a big desk. People who work with a lot of paper or craft items should look for deep, wide desks that can accommodate supplies. Try to position frequently used items within arm's reach, especially when designing a space for someone with limited mobility.

Make sure the desk you choose is a comfortable height and has adequate leg space. Wheelchair users need at least 29" of side-to-side clearance. If you do a lot of computer work, include an adjustable keyboard tray that can be positioned to minimize repetitive strain injuries from typing, especially for people with limited arm or hand strength.

Reduce glare and eyestrain for the elderly and people with limited vision by selecting a desk with a light or medium stain and a matte finish.

Choose desks with rounded, rather than sharp, corners to reduce the chances of bruising.

■ **Wheelchair Modifications:**

- Install an adjustable keyboard tray on your desk.
- Include at least one section of desktop no higher than 32" for roll-under access.

Chairs

The right chair can help you and your family work more comfortably. Even though good quality office chairs are expensive, they are well worth the cost because they reduce the back and neck pain, poor circulation, and fatigue caused by sitting.

Choose an adjustable chair with controls that can be manipulated while seated. Hydraulic lever controls, instead of twist knobs, are best for people with limited hand, arm, or leg strength.

Adjust the chair so you can sit back with your thighs parallel to the floor and your feet flat on the floor. Choose a chair with a "waterfall" back that curves out at the small of the back. A good chair will allow you to adjust the back support's height and position.

Choose a curved, molded seat that is deep and wide enough for the people who will sit in it. The seat should be flat or tilted upward, slightly. A seat that slopes toward the floor will put added pressure on the back and thighs.

The front edge of the seat should be rounded, and the entire seat should be well padded or evenly tensioned if it is mesh. If the chair includes armrests, position them so your arms can sit in your lap without bumping the rests. Make sure the armrests allow your shoulders to sit at their natural height—not raised or slumped.

■ **Wheelchair Modifications:**

- Look for smooth-rolling chairs that can be moved out of the way for wheelchair access.

File Cabinets, Stands & Bookcases

Use carts with smooth-rolling wheels to store printers, fax machines, and hobby equipment at a usable height for people with back injuries or limited

Photo courtesy of Room & Board.

An adjustable chair should have controls that can be manipulated while sitting.

arm strength. Keep seldom-used items and supplies in easily accessed file cabinets with smooth latch mechanisms and drawers to eliminate straining and reaching.

Move reference materials, supplies, and completed hobbies off your desk or floor and into a wall-hung bookcase or a door storage unit to keep floors clear for the elderly and people with vision problems.

Make sure that all carts, cabinets, and bookcases are sturdy and level to reduce the risk of tipping.

■ **Wheelchair & Walker Modifications:**

• Store equipment against the wall to create clear floor space.

• Choose low cabinets with full-extension drawers that are well balanced against tipping.

• Include at least one wall-hung storage unit to free up floor space.

Monitors, Keyboards & Software
Purchase specialty hardware and software, such as screen-reading software, adaptive keyboards, wireless keyboards and mice, voice recognition, and vision enhancers, to compensate for physical limitations. Most major software developers and specialty hardware manufacturers offer adaptive products to meet a variety of needs. Go directly to their Web sites, ask distributors about the variety of products available, or scan the listings in the Resources section at the end of this book.

Choose a computer that fits your family's work style and physical size. Large-screen models, with adjustable monitors and full keyboards, offer the greatest flexibility. Notebook and laptop computers are handy if you travel or work outside the office, but their small monitors and compact keyboards can be very difficult to use for people with vision problems and limited hand mobility.

Swing arms and racks are available to easily move monitors and computers off desktops to make more space for other tasks. A rolling computer cart can free up desk space, make cables more accessible, and allow the computer to be stored when not in use.

Low file cabinets (above) are easier for short people and wheelchair users to access.

Photo courtesy of IKEA.

Flooring
Choose low-pile carpeting or cork, to prevent tripping, for the elderly or people with vision, hearing, or mobility problems. Dense floor coverings absorb sound, offer surer footing, and allow wheelchairs to roll smoothly. Consider a non-static, plastic chair pad under the desk to help people with limited leg strength or mobility problems easily move their chair.

If your hobby creates dust or other debris, look for nonglare, slip-resistant vinyl, tile, or wood flooring that can be easily swept or cleaned.

■ **Wheelchair & Walker Modifications:**

• Replace or remove thresholds that are higher than ½", or use transition wedges.

• Provide level and nonslip floors in vinyl, tile, or wood.

• Choose dense, low-pile carpeting or cork so wheelchairs can roll smoothly.

Ventilation
If you use a copy machine regularly in your home office, or you use solvent-based glues or oil-based paints for your hobbies, you will need to provide

Photo courtesy of Room & Board.

Adjustable keyboard trays can be positioned for individual users to minimize the risk of repetitive strain injuries.

adequate ventilation. Reduce air toxins by opening windows, running the air conditioner, and filtering heated air. A genuine HEPA (high efficiency particulate air) filter removes air pollutants, allergens, and smoke particles. Decorate with real plants to clean the air naturally.

■ **Wheelchair & Walker Modifications:**

- Keep access to windows clear.
- Locate controls for air conditioners and heaters within reach, or automate heating and cooling systems.
- Lower windows and install latches at sill level so they are accessible to seated users.
- Install automated window systems with remote control access.

Wallcoverings

Reduce background noise for people with hearing problems by hanging wallpaper in your office or hobby room. Simple patterns in neutral colors are less distracting for the elderly or people with vision problems. Minimize glare with matte-finish paint in neutral colors.

Phone & Intercom

Choose accessible phone features, such as large, lighted buttons for the elderly and people with vision problems, auto-dial features or voice activation for people with limited hand strength or memory impairment, and cordless operation for people with mobility problems.

Select add-on features to maximize comfort and performance. If neck or back pain is an issue, add a headset to your system. Use a speaker phone to compensate for limited hand strength. When limited mobility makes it difficult to communicate with someone working in the home office or hobby room, install an intercom system throughout the house.

Choose flooring appropriate to the hobby or work you perform. Hobby rooms benefit from easy-clean floors.

GARAGE & UTILITY SPACES

A garage or utility room can serve many purposes in your home: entrance, storage space, hobby room, workshop, lawn and garden center, and car shelter.

Turn these underdeveloped, overworked spaces into well-lit, organized areas so everyone in the family can participate in hobbies, home maintenance, and lawn care in a safe, accessible environment. Mount an automatic door opener to eliminate an obstacle to driving. Install a keyless dead bolt to open entryways to the home. And build an adjustable shelving system to put hobby and workshop items within reach.

Look over the ideas that follow to update lighting and electrical components, improve entrances, and increase function in your garage and utility spaces. The results will increase your home's value and enhance your family's safety.

Photo courtesy of Closetworks.

Garage Doors

Install a garage door opener to lift heavy doors automatically for the elderly or people with limited mobility. Make sure the safety features of existing garage door openers are working properly.

Consider a push-button keypad on an attached garage, so people with limited hand strength can enter the garage entrance without using house keys or doorknobs.

When limited vision is a problem, look for openers that feature bright overhead lights and lighted keypads.

■ **Wheelchair Modifications:**
- Choose an opener with an electronic sensor to prevent the door from closing on a wheelchair.

Entry Doors

Replace or repair warped or sticky exterior garage access doors. To prevent the elderly or people with limited mobility from tripping, ensure thresholds are no higher than ¼", and remove area rugs in mud rooms or secure them with double-stick carpet tape.

Photo courtesy of Handi-Ramp.

Lifts are good options when there isn't enough room to build a ramp. Choose a model rated for outdoor use when you install a lift at an exterior entrance.

Install additional lighting near entrances to eliminate shadows and help the elderly or people with vision problems adjust to changes in light. For convenience, wire lights to go on automatically when someone opens the door.

If limited hand or arm strength is an issue, consider an automatic door opener to open and hold entry doors between the garage and house. Look for models that offer adjustable timing and automatic locking mechanisms for added convenience.

■ **Wheelchair & Walker Modifications:**
- Remove area rugs at entrances.
- Make sure thresholds are no higher than ¼".
- Consider an automatic door opener to open and hold entry doors.

Steps

Paint steps with traction-increasing paint or apply traction strips to stair treads. Consider closing off the back of open riser stairs to make it easier for people with vision problems to gauge stair depth. If the stairs are especially shallow, or no landing at the top of the steps exists, you may want to replace the stairs.

Add a railing to both sides of garage steps to help the elderly or people with mobility problems steady themselves. Choose a round railing that is easy to grip between the thumb and fingers, and install it at a height of 34 to 38". Make sure that railings are rated to support 250 pounds.

A package shelf placed at the top of the railing or next to the door can hold items while family members with limited hand or arm strength unlock and open the door.

If stairs are particularly difficult, consider installing an electric lift or building a ramp. A lift or ramp inside an attached garage will protect family members from the elements while they enter the house, especially during inclement weather.

Check with your local building department regarding codes and regulations before you install any permanent structure inside your garage.

When installing a ramp, be sure to maintain a slope no greater than 1:12 for safety (page 124). Lifts generally require less room than ramps, but be sure to select a model rated for outdoor use.

▣ Wheelchair & Walker Modifications:

- Install a lift or ramp inside the garage.

Lighting & Electrical

Install full-spectrum lightbulbs in overhead fixtures to simulate sunlight and eliminate shadows for people with limited vision.

In workshop areas, add fluorescent or halogen fixtures. Or add adjustable track lighting. Use long-life bulbs to reduce the need for frequent replacement.

New options in lighting can increase your vision in storage areas. Choose fluorescent or halogen lighting to get a bright white light for projects.

For people with limited vision and hand strength, replace standard toggle switches with lighted rocker switches or motion-sensor lights.

If the garage or utility room has more than one entrance, add three-way switches near doors to make lights easily accessible for the elderly or people with mobility problems.

For safety, be sure the garage or utility room has enough receptacles to supply adequate power to electric tools and equipment. Install additional outlets at a minimum height of 18" near the workbench to reduce bending for people with back or mobility problems. Instead of using extension cords, mount additional receptacles and lights where they're needed. Electrical codes require that garage receptacles be GFCI outlets.

As a precaution, install a telephone and intercom in the garage or utility room so disabled family members can answer calls and communicate with other family members in case of emergency.

▣ Wheelchair & Walker Modifications:

- Keep extension cords out of pathways.
- Install outlets 18" above floor level.
- Use three-way switches when the room has more than one entrance.
- Install motion-sensor switches.

Workbenches

Choose a wall-hung workbench with roll-under access, so people with back or leg problems can sit comfortably while working. Place the workbench in an area with the least disruption from cars and other activities.

If limited mobility, reach, or hand strength is a problem, store tools and equipment on pegboard attached to the side of the workbench or use rolling storage units to keep supplies handy. Use hot glue to secure pegboard hooks so they don't fall out.

Install electrical receptacles or a power strip at an easy-to-reach height to minimize bending and reaching.

▣ Wheelchair & Walker Modifications:

- Use rolling storage units for easy access to supplies.
- Hang pegboard to the side of the workbench to eliminate reaching.
- Choose a wall-hung workbench with roll-under access at least 29" wide and a work surface no higher than 32".
- Include a fold-down panel of outlets on the front of the workbench.

A tidy, well-organized workbench makes work safer and more comfortable. Consider a wall-hung unit for wheelchair access.

Storage

Use clear storage bins so people with limited hand strength can see supplies without having to lift and move bins.

Use C-shaped drawer and cupboard handles or magnetic touch latches for easy access.

Keep floors clear for the elderly and people with limited vision or mobility by using storage cabinets. Enclosed cabinets with interior lighting create a finished appearance and are easy to use.

Store lawn and garden supplies on rolling carts and hooks near entrances so people with back injuries or limited arm strength can access them easily.

Include at least one set of open, adjustable shelves (page 108) so boxes, decorations, and other items can be stored within reach.

Repair cracks in garage or utility room concrete floors to prevent tripping and allow smooth rolling for wheelchairs and walkers.

■ **Wheelchair Modifications:**
• Mount hooks no higher than 32".
• Choose short storage cabinets with shallow, adjustable shelves.
• Store equipment and supplies in rolling storage units.
• Use adjustable shelving with open space underneath.

Floor

To prevent the elderly or people with mobility problems from tripping, repair cracks in concrete floors and clean up debris and scraps quickly. Use traction paint or adhesive traction strips to prevent slipping in areas that might get wet.

To prevent back strain and leg fatigue, use rubber mats, carpet scraps or cardboard in front of the workbench or other work areas. Secure floor coverings with double-sided carpet tape to prevent tripping.

If limited vision is a problem, consider painting the floor a light color in a matte finish to reflect light, reduce glare, and brighten the work area.

■ **Wheelchair & Walker Modifications:**
• Make sure floors are level and have a non-slip surface.
• Provide at least 5 ft. of clear space for turning.
• Repair cracks in concrete to provide smooth rolling for wheelchairs.

Ventilation

Garages need to be properly ventilated, especially if you are using solvents or storing gasoline or other flammables. Make sure windows are functional and easy to access. Or install vents or an exhaust fan.

■ **Wheelchair & Walker Modifications:**
• Keep access to windows clear.
• Locate controls for vent fans within reach.
• Lower windows and install latches at sill level so they are accessible to seated users.

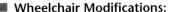

Photo courtesy of Lillian Vernon.

Mount hanging wall systems at an accessible height to keep lawn, garden, and sports equipment off the floor and prevent tripping.

Use rolling recycling containers to eliminate lifting.

Customize prefabricated workbenches with adjustable shelves and hanging rack systems. Create roll-under or seated access by removing a low workbench shelf.

GARAGE DOOR OPENER

A garage door can hinder independence for people with limited mobility or back injuries by making cars, tools, and lawn equipment inaccessible.

An automatic garage door opener can eliminate the daily struggle to get into and out of the garage. Special features like keyless entry systems provide secure access without keys or doorknobs and electronic sensors prevent people or items from being crushed under the door.

There are three basic models of garage door openers: chain drives, belt drives, and screw drives. Chain drives are the most common and inexpensive, but they can be noisy. Belt drives are quiet but expensive. The slow, smooth operation of screw drives make them ideal for one-piece doors that are best opened slowly.

Garage door opener wireless remote controllers come in a variety of forms. You can get keychain versions, visor clip-on units, and keyless entry touchpads. If you are purchasing additional remote controllers, make certain the frequency matches your opener.

This project shows you the basic steps for installing a chain drive system on a sectional door in a garage with exposed joists.

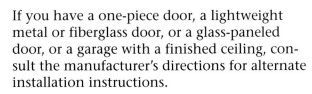

Photo courtesy of The Genie Company.

If you have a one-piece door, a lightweight metal or fiberglass door, or a glass-paneled door, or a garage with a finished ceiling, consult the manufacturer's directions for alternate installation instructions.

Before you begin, make sure your garage door is properly balanced and moves smoothly. The garage door opener does not support the garage door and the opener motor will be damaged by being attached to a poorly operating door. Open and close the door to see if it sticks or binds at any point. Release the door in the half-open position. It should stay in place, supported by its own springs.

If your door is not balanced or if it sticks, call a garage door service professional before attempting to install an opener. Garage door springs and cables are under extreme tension and can cause serious injury if improperly released or stressed to the breaking point.

Most garage door openers plug into a standard grounded receptacle located near the unit, but some local codes require openers to be hard-wired. If you plan to hard-wire your opener, consult the manufacturer's directions.

HOW TO INSTALL A GARAGE DOOR OPENER

STEP A: *Align & Secure Rails*

1. Align the rail pieces in proper order and secure them with the included braces and bolts.

2. Screw the pulley bracket to the door-end of the rail and slide the trolley onto the rail. Make sure the pulley and all rail pieces are properly aligned and that the trolley runs smoothly without hitting any hardware along the rail.

3. Remove the two screws from the top of the opener, then attach the rail to the opener using those screws.

STEP B: *Attach the Drive Chain/Cable*

1. Attach the cable loop to the front of the trolley using the included linking hardware.

2. Wrap the cable around the pulley, then wrap the remaining chain around the drive sprocket on the opener.

3. Attach the chain to the other side of the trolley with the linking hardware. Make sure the chain is not twisted, then attach the cover over the drive sprocket. Tighten the chain by adjusting the nuts on the trolley until the chain is ½" above the base of the rail.

STEP C: *Fasten the Header Bracket*

1. Locate the header bracket position, by extending a vertical line from the center of the door onto the wall above.

2. Raise the door and note the highest point it reaches. Measure from the floor to this point, and add 2" to this distance. Then mark a horizontal line on the front wall where it intersects the centerline.

3. If there is no structural support behind the cross point, fasten 2× lumber across the framing. Then

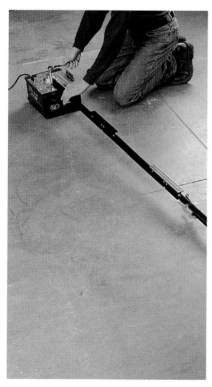

A. *Align the rail pieces in order and secure them with the included bolts and braces. Then attach the rail to the opener.*

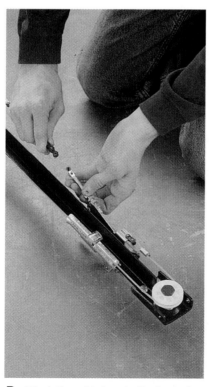

B. *Attach the cable loop to the front of the trolley with the linking hardware.*

C. *Secure the header bracket above the door. If there is no structural support present, fasten 2× lumber across the framing.*

D. *Attach the rail pulley bracket to the header bracket above the door with the included clevis pin.*

fasten the header bracket to the structural support with the included screws.

STEP D: *Attach Rail Pulley to Header Bracket*

1. Support the opener on the floor with a board or box to prevent stressing and possibly twisting the rail.

2. Attach the rail pulley bracket to the header bracket above the door with the included clevis pin.

3. Place the opener on a stepladder so it is above the door tracks. Open the door and shim beneath the opener, until the rail is 2" above the door.

STEP E: *Hang the Opener*

1. Hang the opener from the ceiling joists with the included hanging brackets and screws. Angle at least one of the hanging brackets to ensure stability. If the ceiling joists run parallel to the door, nail two lengths of 2 × 4 between the joists and attach the opener to these.

2. Attach the manual release cord and handle to the release arm of the trolley.

STEP F: *Connect the Opener to the Wall Console*

1. Strip ¼" of sheathing from the wall-console bell

E. *Place the opener on a stepladder, then attach the opener to the hanging brackets. Angle at least one bracket to ensure stability.*

F. *Run wires from the wall console to the opener along the inside wall of the garage, and connect the wires to the proper terminals on the opener.*

wire, and connect the wire to the screw terminals on the console.

2. Attach the wall console to the inside wall of the garage at a convenient location with the included screws, and run the wire to the opener.

3. Connect the wires to the proper terminals on the opener.

4. Secure the wire to the wall with insulated staples, being careful not to pierce the wire.

5. Install the lightbulbs and lenses.

STEP G: *Install the Sensor Eye*

1. Install the sensor eye mounting brackets at each side of the garage door, parallel to each other, about 4 to 6" from the floor. The sensor brackets can be attached to the door track, the wall, or the floor, depending upon your garage layout. See the manufacturer's directions for the best configuration for your garage.

2. Attach the sensor eyes to the brackets with the included wing nuts, but do not tighten the nuts completely. Make sure the path between the sensor eyes is unobstructed by the door tracks or other items.

3. Run wires from both sensors to the opener unit and connect the wires to the proper terminals.

4. Plug the opener into the grounded receptacle and adjust the sensors until the indicator light shows correct eye alignment. Then tighten the wing nuts.

5. Unplug the unit and attach the sensor wires to the walls with insulated staples.

STEP H: *Connect the Door Bracket*

1. Center the door bracket 2 to 4" below the top of the door. Drill holes and attach the bracket with the included carriage bolts.

2. Connect the straight and curved arm sections with the included bolts, then attach the arm to the trolley and door bracket with the included latch pins.

3. Plug the opener into a grounded receptacle and test the unit. See the manufacturer's directions for making adjustments and testing the sensor function. Follow the manufacturer's instructions for mounting an external wireless keypad.

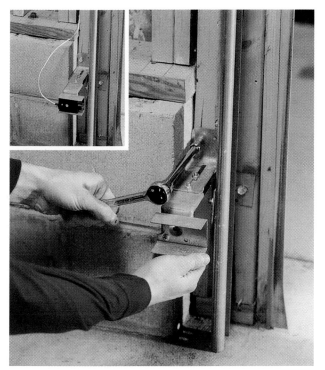

G. *Install the sensor eye mounting brackets at each side of the door, parallel to each other, on either the door track, the wall, or the floor, depending upon your garage layout. Then attach the sensor eyes to the brackets (inset), and wire them to the opener.*

H. *Drill holes and attach the door bracket 2 to 4" below the top of the door. Connect the arm to the door bracket with a latch pin.*

KEYLESS DEAD-BOLT LOCK

Keyless entry systems provide home security with a custom code or remote, rather than a key, which makes them a good choice for people with limited hand strength.

Most keyless systems are easy to install. However, if you are replacing an old dead bolt with a keyless entry system, don't assume the new lock will fit the existing holes. If the door and jamb holes are slightly misaligned, the lock will not work properly. Consult the manufacturer's directions for measurement requirements.

HOW TO INSTALL A KEYLESS DEAD BOLT
STEP A: *Drill Pilot Holes*
1. Tape the manufacturer's template to your door in the desired location, usually about 5½" above the existing lockset.

TOOLS & MATERIALS

- Awl
- Drill with ⅛" bit
- Hole saw
- Spade bits
- Utility knife
- Hammer
- Chisel
- Flat-head and Phillips screwdrivers
- Keyless entry dead-bolt kit
- Nail
- 3" wood screws

2. Mark the center positions for the cylinder and dead-bolt holes, using an awl.
3. Drill pilot holes at the marked points entirely through the door face and 2" into the door edge.
STEP B: *Bore Cylinder Hole*
1. Use a drill and hole saw to bore the cylinder hole through the door. To avoid splintering the wood, drill through one side of the door until the pilot bit comes through, then finish drilling the hole from the other side.
STEP C: *Bore the Strike Box & Latch Holes*
1. Mark the center of the strike box onto the door jamb by closing the door and pressing a nail from inside the cylinder hole through the pilot hole in the door edge, until it marks the door jamb.
2. Use the recommended size of spade bit to bore a 1"-deep hole into the jamb.
3. Bore the dead-bolt latch hole through the door edge and into the cylinder hole.
STEP D: *Install the Dead-bolt Latch*
1. Insert the dead-bolt latch into the door edge and secure it temporarily with the included screws.
2. Score around the faceplate with a utility knife. Remove the latch and chisel within the scored lines until the faceplate fits flush with the door.
3. Attach the dead-bolt latch to the door with the included screws.
STEP E: *Install the Strike Box*
1. Insert the strike box into the door jamb. Make sure the dead-bolt is precisely aligned with the strike plate. Chisel out a recess so the strike plate is flush with the

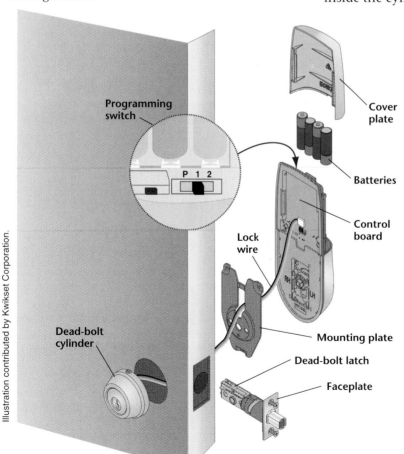

Programming switch

Cover plate

Batteries

P 1 2

Control board

Lock wire

Mounting plate

Dead-bolt cylinder

Dead-bolt latch

Faceplate

Illustration contributed by Kwikset Corporation.

jamb, as in step D.

2. Drill pilot holes, and install the strike plate with 3" wood screws.

STEP F: *Fit the Lock*

1. Fit the cylinder into its hole so the tailpiece runs through the proper hole on the dead-bolt latch.

2. Route the lock wire underneath the latch, making sure it is free of any moving parts. Run the wire through the interior mounting plate, and attach the plate to the latch with the included screws.

3. Follow the manufacturer's instructions to set the lock for a left- or right-hand door. Plug the lock wire into the interior control board receiving wire.

4. With the bolt extended and the knob in the vertical position, slide the board into place and attach it with the included screws.

5. Install the batteries, then program the remote and entry codes.

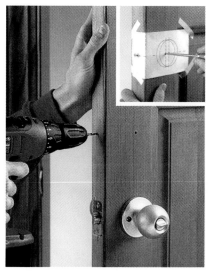

A. *Use the template and an awl to mark the cylinder and dead-bolt holes (inset). Drill pilot holes at the marked locations.*

B. *Cut the cylinder hole with a hole saw. Drill until the pilot bit comes through, then complete the hole from the other side.*

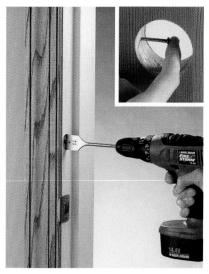

C. *Mark the center of the strike box onto the door jamb (inset), then bore the strike plate hole into the door jamb.*

D. *Score around the latch faceplate (inset), then chisel out a recess so the faceplate is flush with the door edge.*

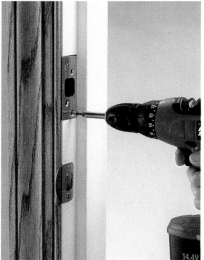

E. *Chisel out a recess for the strike plate and secure it to the jamb and door framing with 3" wood screws.*

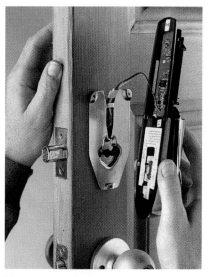

F. *Install the cylinder, and interior mounting plate. Plug the lock wire into the control board wire. Then install the control board.*

ADJUSTABLE UTILITY SHELVES

Adjustable utility shelves put storage items within reach for both standing and seated family members. When the bottom shelf of this unit is raised and the floor space is kept clear, it provides convenient roll-under access for wheelchair users.

The project shown here can be built in a single afternoon, using 2 × 4s and ¾" plywood. This unit has two shelf columns, with a total width of 68". You can enlarge the project by adding more 2 × 4 risers and plywood shelves. (For strength, do not increase the individual shelf widths to more than 36".)

TOOLS & MATERIALS

- Tape measure
- Studfinder
- Level
- Framing square
- Drill

- Plumb bob
- Clamps
- 2 × 4 lumber
- ¾" plywood
- Router with ¾" straight bit

- Circular saw
- Wood glue
- Shims (if needed)
- 2½" & 3" screws
- Construction adhesive

EXPLODED VIEW OF UTILITY SHELVES

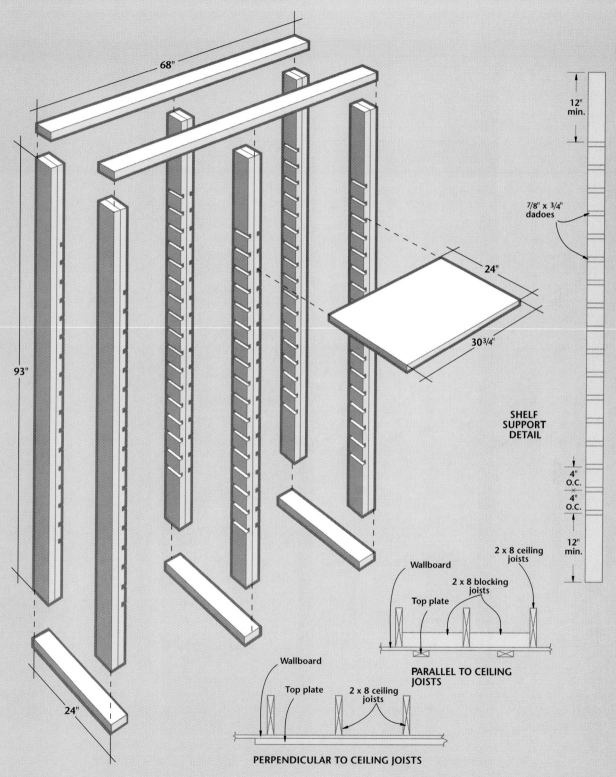

68"

93"

24"

24"

SHELF
SUPPORT
DETAIL

12"
min.

7/8" x 3/4"
dadoes

24"

30 3/4"

4"
O.C.

4"
O.C.

12"
min.

Wallboard

2 x 8 ceiling
joists

2 x 8 blocking
joists

Top plate

**PARALLEL TO CEILING
JOISTS**

Wallboard

Top plate

2 x 8 ceiling
joists

PERPENDICULAR TO CEILING JOISTS

HOW TO BUILD ADJUSTABLE UTILITY SHELVES

STEP A: *Install the Plates*

1. Determine whether the ceiling joists are parallel or perpendicular to your shelf project, using a studfinder. Mark the joist locations. If the joists are parallel to your project, you will need to attach the top plates to the joists—which will dictate the distance from the wall for the top plate—or install blocking between joists. (See diagram on page 109.)

2. Mark the location for the top plates on the ceiling. Position one plate flush against the wall. Position the other plate parallel to the first, with its front edge 24" from the wall.

3. Cut the 2 × 4 top plates to size, then fasten them to the ceiling joists or blocking with 3" screws. Do not secure the plates to the ceiling drywall only.

4. Using a plumb bob, mark the points directly beneath the outside corners of the top plates to locate the position of the outer bottom plates.

5. Make reference lines for the bottom plates by drawing lines perpendicular to the wall connecting each pair of points.

6. Cut outer 2 × 4 bottom plates and position them perpendicular to the wall, just inside the outlines. If necessary, shim the plates to make them level. If the floor is bare concrete, use pressure-treated lumber for the bottom plates.

7. Apply construction adhesive to the floor. Then attach the outer bottom plates to the floor with a powder-actuated nailer or 3" masonry screws.

8. Attach a center bottom plate midway between the outer bottom plates.

STEP B: *Cut the Shelf Risers*

1. Prepare the shelf risers by cutting ⅞"-wide × ¾"-deep dadoes with a router. Cut dadoes every 4" along the inside face of each 2 × 4 riser, with the top and bottom dadoes cut about 12" from the ends of the 2 × 4.

To save time, gang-cut the risers: Lay them flat and clamp them together so their top faces are flush, then attach a cutting jig or straightedge to guide

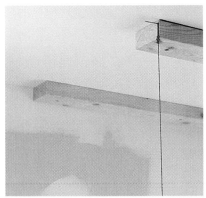

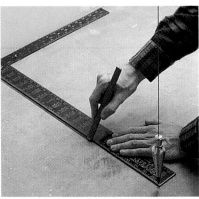

A. *Cut top plates to size, and attach them to ceiling joists or blocking. Plumb down from the top plates to mark the bottom plate locations.*

B. *Cut dadoes into the shelf risers using a router and cutting jig. Cut the risers to length before unclamping them.*

the router. For each cut, make several passes with the router, gradually increasing the bit depth until the dadoes are ¾" deep.

2. Measure the distance between the top and bottom plates. Use a circular saw and a cutting jig or straightedge to trim the shelf risers to length before unclamping them. In order to have all the shelf support dadoes line up, make a note of which end will be the top. Make sure that you assemble and install all the shelf supports with the same orientation.

STEP C: *Assemble the Shelf Supports*

1. Build two center shelf supports by positioning pairs of dadoed shelf risers back-to-back and joining them with wood glue and 2½" screws.

2. Build four end shelf supports by positioning the back of a dadoed shelf riser against a 2 × 4 of the same length, then joining the pieces with glue and 2½" screws.

STEP D: *Install the Supports*

1. Position an end shelf support at each corner of the shelving unit, between the top and bottom plates. Attach the supports by driving 3" screws at an angle into the top plate and bottom plates.

2. Position a center shelf support (both faces dadoed) at each end of the center bottom plate. Anchor the shelf supports to the bottom plate, using 3" screws driven at an angle.

3. Use a framing square to align the center shelf supports perpendicular to the top plates, then anchor them to the top plates with screws.

STEP E: *Cut & Install the Shelves*

1. To determine the width of the shelves, measure the distance between facing dado grooves, then subtract ¼". To find the shelf depth, measure from the back wall to the front edges of the shelf supports. Cut plywood shelves to fit.

2. Slide the shelves into the grooves. Applying beeswax to the shelf edges will make them slide more easily.

C. *Build two center shelf supports (top) by joining pairs of shelf risers. Build four end shelf supports (bottom) by joining a dadoed shelf riser and a 2 × 4 of the same length.*

D. *Fasten the shelf supports to the top and bottom plates, using screws. Drive the screws at an angle through each support and into the plate (inset).*

E. *Measure between the shelf supports and cut the shelves to fit. Install the shelves by sliding them into the dadoes.*

OUTDOORS

ardening and outdoor entertaining bring nature close to home and enrich the spirit with a sense of freedom and well-being.

Enjoy your yard and patio again by incorporating some easy ideas for accessibility into your landscaping plan. Care for lawn and gardens by installing a raised garden spigot. Increase nighttime safety on patios, walking paths, and sidewalks with a combination of floodlights, spotlights, and landscape lighting. In addition, discover products that take the agony out of outdoor maintenance, and learn how to make gardening more comfortable with raised beds and planters.

The ideas that follow will help you create multi-level landscapes and patio gardens so the whole family can enjoy communing with nature and gathering with friends outdoors.

Walkways

Keep concrete sidewalks level and in good repair. If cracks have appeared, use ready-mix concrete to patch them. If slabs have settled or moved apart, jack them up and level them with sand and gravel.

Pull or kill weeds growing in walkways to prevent tripping for the elderly and for people with limited vision or mobility. In areas with extreme winters, consider installing an ice-thawing system to keep walkways clear.

Lay concrete or brick walkways from the garage to the front door and from the front entrance to the back door. A boardwalk with slats spaced no more than ¼" apart is another walkway option for your home. Avoid materials that can be slippery when wet, especially for people with mobility problems.

All walkways should be at least 36" wide, but consider increasing the width to 48 to 54" so someone can walk next to an elderly or disabled family member to provide support.

Erect handrails on one or both sides of walkways. Make sure they can support 250 pounds.

Include benches as part of your walkway design so that people with limited strength can sit and rest while outdoors.

■ Wheelchair & Walker Modifications:

• Pull or kill weeds growing in sidewalks.

• Repair cracks in concrete, and level slabs that have settled or moved apart.

• Build boardwalks with slats spaced no more than ¼" apart.

• Consider an ice-thaw system to keep walkways clear in winter.

Entryways

Provide level outdoor entryways, with thresholds no higher than ¼" for the elderly or people with limited vision or mobility. When deck and patio thresholds are higher than the recommended height, remove them, replace them, or add a threshold ramp for accessibility.

Light entryways and install overhangs to protect people with limited vision and mobility from the elements while they open the door. Consider a keyless entry system (page 106) for family members with limited hand strength.

■ Wheelchair & Walker Modifications:

• Make sure thresholds are no higher than ¼" or use a threshold ramp for accessibility.

• Add a ramp to exterior entrances (page 124).

Keep walkways in good repair to prevent tripping and falls. Patch and lift uneven sidewalks, pull or kill weeds, and keep walkways clear of snow, ice, leaves, and debris.

Lighting & Electrical

Use a variety of lighting to enhance safety and visibility. Install floodlights (page 122) to illuminate patio areas, hang overhead lighting to eliminate glare, use spotlights to light up keyholes, and add landscape lighting (page 120) near walkways, decks, and patios to prevent falls and help people with vision problems mark boundaries.

Automatic sensor lighting provides convenience and security for people with limited memory, vision, or mobility. Fit fixtures with long-life lightbulbs to reduce bulb replacement for people with mobility problems, and choose full-spectrum bulbs to enhance visibility for people with limited vision.

Include accessible receptacles in your outdoor plans. Place outlets at least 18" above the deck or patio floor to prevent bending and stretching for people with back or joint problems.

For people with mobility or hearing problems, install a phone jack on the deck or patio—or keep a cordless or cell phone handy—so family members can answer calls easily. Wire the doorbell to ring on outside patios or decks.

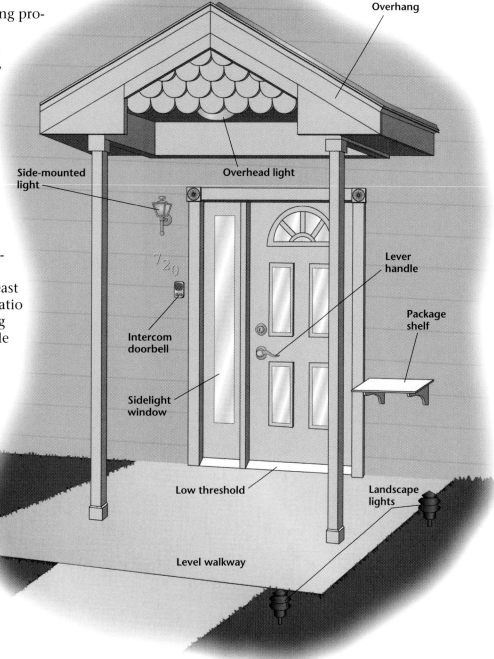

An accessible entryway combines adequate lighting with convenience features.

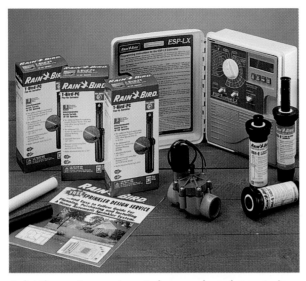

Irrigation systems automate lawn and garden watering for the elderly and people with mobility problems.

■ **Wheelchair & Walker Modifications:**
- Use long-life bulbs in light fixtures.
- Place outlets at least 18" above the deck or patio floor.
- Install motion-sensor floodlights.

Planters & Gardens

To help people with vision problems mark boundaries, include multi-level elements in your garden. Plant flowers and bushes along sidewalks to mark walkways, and add trellises and arbors to mark edges of decks and patios. When placed properly, these garden accessories also will provide shade and reduce glare for people with vision problems or sun sensitivity.

Build raised garden and flower beds so people with back injuries or limited reach can garden without bending or stretching. A roll-under

elevated garden bed or potting table allows wheelchair or seated access.

Hang deck-railing planters to put flowers and vegetables at eye level for seated gardeners. Or, install a raised water garden or fountain. Consult a local gardening supply center and pet store for water gardens, plants, and fish that are suitable for your area.

■ **Wheelchair & Walker Modifications:**
  • Include raised garden beds or deck railing planters on your deck and patio.
  • Consider a raised water garden or fountain.

Watering
Install a raised garden spigot (page 118) near a patio or walkway, so people with limited mobility can reach it for watering.

Install soaker hoses or consider an automated irrigation system for use by the elderly and people with limited mobility.

■ **Wheelchair & Walker Modifications:**
  • Install a raised hose bib for watering.
  • Consider an automated irrigation system.

Shaded Areas
For people with light sensitivity, limited vision, or reduced mobility, include shaded areas in your outdoor design.

Install an overhang at your entryway to shade family and guests as they enter and leave

Photo courtesy of CertainTeed EverNew

Vinyl fencing materials provide privacy and shade, without maintenance worries.

your home. Mount an automated retractable awning over your deck or patio area to provide shade at the touch of a button.

To add beauty, as well as shade, include trellises and arbors planted with vines and flowers near your deck or patio. Plant well-placed trees to produce midday shadows.

■ **Wheelchair & Walker Modifications:**
  • Install automated awnings with controls mounted no higher than 32".

Fences, Decking & Siding
Install maintenance-free fencing, decking, and siding products to eliminate annual painting and scraping for the elderly and people with mobility problems.

Furniture
Select outdoor furniture that can withstand the elements so the elderly and people with limited mobility can leave items outdoors year-round. Look for styles, such as mesh or wrought iron, that are fast drying and treated to prevent fading and mold growth.

Avoid chairs that rock or swivel if limited mobility or leg strength is a problem. For people with vision problems, choose upholstery in simple patterns and neutral colors.

MAIL-ARRIVAL INDICATORS

Getting the mail can be a daily challenge for people with limited mobility, especially when the mailbox is located at the end of a driveway or in a neighborhood depot box. There's nothing worse than making your way to the mailbox to discover the mail hasn't arrived yet.

Now it's possible to know if mail has arrived before you go outside. Electronic and manual indicators alert you to mail arrival. Some devices are decorative and rest on top of the mailbox. Others are electronic devices that send a signal to a home monitor.

Mount a decorative indicator where it can be seen from inside your home. Check the signal range on an electronic device. Before installing any device on your box, consult your local post office or mail carrier.

RAISED GARDEN SPIGOT

Adding a raised garden spigot to your garden puts water near your plants and eliminates the bending and reaching associated with spigots located on your home's foundation.

The project shown here can be located almost anywhere in your yard. To install it, you'll have to run a branch line from your home's water supply system, through the foundation or exterior wall, and along an underground trench to a hose spigot anchored to a post, which is embedded in a bucket of concrete. If limited hand strength is an issue, fit the spigot with an accessible lever handle.

In this project, copper pipe is used for the aboveground sections of the run and polyethylene (PE) pipe is used for the buried sections. Your local plumbing code may have other requirements for pipe materials. Check with local authorities before you begin, and be sure to acquire permits and arrange for inspections, if necessary.

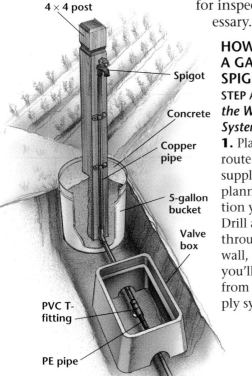

HOW TO INSTALL A GARDEN SPIGOT

STEP A: *Connect to the Water Supply System*

1. Plan a convenient route from the water supply line to the planned spigot location you've chosen. Drill a 1" hole through the exterior wall, near where you'll run the pipe from the water supply system to the valve box. Turn off the water at the main supply valve near the water meter, and drain the water from the pipe.

2. Cut away a small section of the cold water pipe with a tubing cutter, and install a T-fitting. Install a straight length of copper pipe, then a gate valve with a bleed fitting.

3. Use straight lengths of pipe and elbow fittings to extend the branch line through the hole in the wall, installing a vacuum breaker at a convenient point along the way.

STEP B: *Lay Out Branch Line & Install Valve Box*

1. Outside the house, stake a line marking the path for the pipe run to the spigot location.

2. Use a trenching spade to remove sod for an

A. *Tie into your water supply, and install a vacuum breaker at a convenient point along your line.*

8 to 12"-wide trench along the marked route. Dig a trench at least 10" deep and sloping toward the house at a rate of ⅛" per foot.

3. Dig a hole for a valve box, directly below the point where the branch line exits the house.

4. Measure, cut, and attach copper pipe and elbows, extending the branch line down to the bottom of the trench and out 12".

5. Install a valve box with the top flush to the ground. Lay a 4" layer of gravel in the bottom of the valve box.

STEP C: *Run the Supply Line to the Spigot Location*

1. Dig a hole at the spigot location, sized to hold a valve box and bucket. Install the other valve box.

2. Lay ¾" PE pipe in the trench, running from the valve box by the house to the valve box at the spigot location. Use couplings and stainless steel clamps when necessary to join two lengths of pipe.

STEP D: *Install the Spigot*

1. Cut a 3-ft. piece of copper pipe and secure it to one side of the 4 × 4 post, using pipe straps. Mount the spigot on the top of the pipe, then attach an elbow to the bottom of the pipe.

2. Use a drill and spade bit to drill a 1" hole in the side of a 5-gallon bucket, 1" above the bottom.

3. Position the post in the bucket, with the pipe facing toward the hole. Measure, cut, and attach a length of pipe to the elbow at the bottom of the post, extending the pipe through the hole in the bucket and out into the valve box.

4. Place the bucket and post in the hole, with the pipe extending into the valve box. Fill the bucket

with concrete. Use a level to make sure the post is plumb, then let the concrete dry.

5. Install a barbed T-fitting with a threaded outlet, opening facing down, to the PE pipe inside the valve box. Cap the threaded opening with a plug.

6. Using male and female threaded adapters, join the copper pipe to the PE pipe.

7. Repeat steps 1 and 2 to join the pipes in the valve box located near the house. Restore the water and check the line for leaks. Make any necessary adjustments, then refill the trenches. Replace the sod, tamp it down with a shovel, and water it well. Drain the pipes in the winter to prevent bursting.

B. *Extend the branch line through the wall and down into the trench. Install the valve box.*

C. *Lay a run of PE pipe along the bottom of the trench, joining the sections with stainless steel clamps and insert couplings.*

D. *Set the post into the bucket, and fill the bucket with concrete. Join the copper and PE pipe inside the valve boxes (inset).*

OUTDOOR LIGHTING

Install a combination of outdoor lighting fixtures around your home to enhance night-time visibility and safety, especially for people with limited vision.

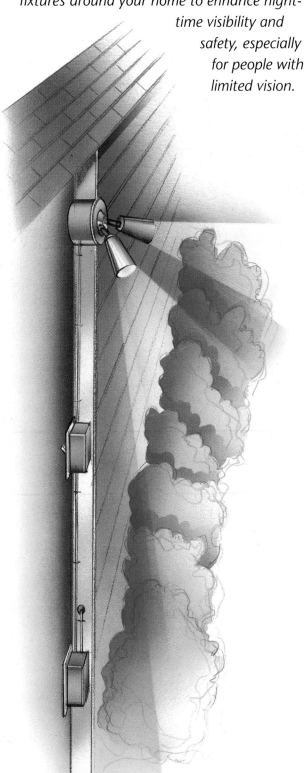

Landscape lighting is available in many different styles and provides low-voltage illumination for your outdoor home. Position lights along stairs, pathways, entrances, patios, and driveways to help people with vision problems mark boundaries.

Most systems are quite simple and easy to install, consisting of the fixtures, low-voltage connector cable, cable connector caps, and a control box containing the low-voltage power transformer. The system plugs into a standard-voltage GFCI receptacle. The project on the following page shows how to install a typical low-voltage lighting system.

Landscape lighting is also available in solar powered models. Though the light is not as bright as wired systems, the installation is very simple because you place the lights where you want them with no digging or wiring.

Floodlights illuminate larger outdoor spaces and help eliminate shadows around patios and house and garage entrances. Motion-sensor fixtures offer additional convenience and safety for people with limited vision or mobility.

The floodlight project on pages 122 to 123 shows how to install a floodlight onto a garage wall, connecting the light switch and fixture to a GFCI receptacle inside the garage. Call your local building department to learn about wiring and permit requirements before starting your project.

When installing floodlights, be considerate of your neighbors. Use only the minimum number of fixtures, make sure the lights are not directed into neighbors' yards or windows, and carefully set motion detectors so that animals or windblown vegetation are not activating them.

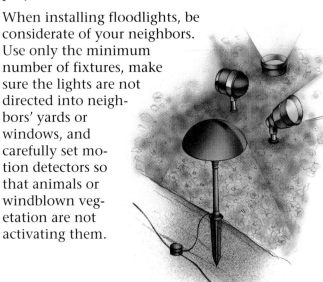

HOW TO INSTALL LANDSCAPE LIGHTING

STEP A: *Mount the Control Box*

1. Mount the control box on an outside wall, near a GFCI receptacle. Make sure the box won't be covered by plants or any other material and is easily accessible.

2. Dig a narrow trench for the light cable, about 6 to 8" deep, using a trenching spade. Start directly beneath the control box and extend the trench about 1 ft. from the wall.

3. Measure from the control box to the bottom of the trench and cut a section of PVC conduit to this length.

4. Feed the cable through the conduit, then position the conduit against the wall, with its bottom resting in the trench. Secure the conduit to the wall with pipe straps.

STEP B: *Run the Cable & Connect the Lights*

1. Starting at the end of the conduit, lay the cable along the ground. Since you'll need to bury the cable, select a path with few obstacles.

2. Assemble each fixture according to the manufacturer's directions.

3. Place each fixture by driving its pointed end into the ground. Attach the fixture to the cable by tightening the cable connector cap, piercing the cable (follow the manufacturer's directions). Repeat to install the remaining fixtures.

4. Plug in the system to turn on the lights and check the fixture placement. Make adjustments, if necessary.

STEP C: *Bury the Cable*

1. Beginning at the trench beneath the control box, dig a narrow trench, about 6 to 8" deep, along the cable path. Also dig a small trench for each branch wire leading to the individual fixtures.

2. Lay the cable into the trench, replace the soil, and gently tamp the soil. Water the sod to help it recover from being disturbed.

A. *Mount the control box on an outside wall, near a GFCI receptacle.*

B. *Stake each fixture, and connect it to the cable with a connector cap.*

C. *Check the fixture positions, then bury the cable in a trench.*

TOOLS & MATERIALS

- Hammer
- Jig saw
- Cable ripper
- Wire combination tool
- Screwdriver
- Plastic light fixture box
- Plastic switch box
- 14-gauge NM cable
- Cable staples
- Floodlight with hardware
- Wire connectors
- Single pole switch

HOW TO INSTALL A FLOODLIGHT

STEP A: *Install the Fixture Box*

1. Turn off the power to the GFCI receptacle to which you'll be wiring the floodlight.

2. Mark the position for the fixture box against the inside of the garage wall, adjacent to a stud.

3. Drill a pilot hole, then cut the hole with a jig saw.

4. Attach the box to the stud with the premounted nails.

STEP B: *Install the Switch Box & Run the Cable*

1. Attach the switch box to a stud near the GFCI.

2. Run one NM cable from the fixture to the switch and another from the switch to the receptacle, allowing an extra 12" at each end. Anchor the cables to the framing with cable staples (staple 8" from each box and every 4 ft. in between).

3. Strip 10" of sheathing from the cable ends and ¾" of insulation from the wires.

STEP C: *Wire the Light Fixture*

1. Open a knockout in the fixture box, and insert the cable into the box.

2. Assemble the light fixture.

3. Attach a bare copper grounding wire to the grounding screw on the fixture. From outside, join the circuit grounding wire to the fixture grounding wire, using a wire connector. Join the white circuit wire to the white fixture wire. Join the black wires.

STEP D: *Connect the Switch*

1. Open knockouts on the top and bottom of the switch box and insert the cables.

2. Attach a copper pigtail to the grounding screw on the switch. Connect the two grounding wires from the cables to the pigtail, using wire connectors. Connect each of the two black wires to the one screw terminal on the switch. Join the two white wires with a wire connector.

3. Tuck the wires inside the box, secure the switch, and install the coverplate.

A. *Cut a hole for the fixture box, then attach the box to a stud by hammering in the premounted nails.*

B. *Attach the switch box to a stud near the receptacle, and run the cables between the fixture, switch, and receptacle boxes.*

Sidelighting uses a series of small, horizontally mounted spotlights to light a surface.

Solar-powered landscape lights offer the convenience of no wiring. They are fitted with rechargeable batteries, powered by the sun.

Photos courtesy of Intermatic Malibu Lighting.

STEP E: *Connect the GFCI Receptacle*

1. Remove the GFCI receptacle from the box, and insert the cable into a knockout. Join the grounding pigtail on the GFCI to both circuit grounding wires, using a wire connector. Attach the wires from the power source to the LINE terminals on the GFCI: the white wire to the silver terminal, and the black to the brass terminal. Attach the wires running from the switch to the LOAD terminals on the GFCI: white to silver and black to brass.
2. Tuck the wires back into the box, secure the receptacle, and install the coverplate.
3. Restore the power and test the light.

C. *Assemble the light fixture, and connect the circuit wires to the fixture wires.*

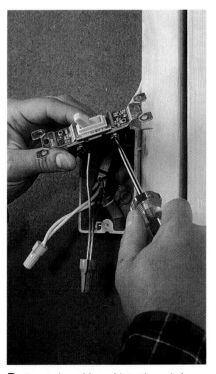

D. *Insert the cable end into the switch box, then wire the switch.*

E. *Remove the GFCI receptacle from the box to connect the new cable.*

RAMPS & LIFTS

Add a ramp of gently sloping concrete, wood, brick, or grass or install an electric lift to make front, side, or back home entrances accessible for a family member who uses a wheelchair or has limited leg or ankle strength.

Consider personal needs, construction costs, and home aesthetics to decide if a ramp or lift is best for you.

Each ramp installation is unique. It's important to consider the abilities of the person for whom you are building the ramp, what future needs the person may have, how much money you have to spend, whether you want the ramp to be permanent, and what type of impact a ramp will have on your home's appearance and market value.

Contact your local building department for permit requirements and construction guidelines. Your state or city may not have codes for residential ramp installations. In that case, commercial ramp guidelines can be helpful in planning your project. The elements listed below are considerations common to any ramp project.

Slope

For safety and function, a ramp slope should not exceed 1:12—meaning it should descend 1 foot for every 12 feet of length. Commercial code requires a much gentler slope of 1:20. Choose a slope for your ramp based on your family members' needs. While it's true that a steeper slope will save you money in materials, it also can create a ramp that's hazardous or unusable for someone using a wheelchair or walker.

Gentler slopes mean longer ramps. Switchbacks or landings in your design will add to your ramp's length.

Determine Ramp Rise & Run

The rise of your ramp will determine the necessary run, or length, of your ramp. Using a string and a line level, determine the rise between the doorsill and the end of the walkway. Drive a stake into the ground at the end of the walkway. Attach a string to the doorsill and the stake, level the string, and measure the height of the string at the stake. This is the rise.

Multiplying the rise by the second number in your desired slope ratio will give you the ramp length. For example, if the rise is 15" and you have chosen a 1:12 ramp slope, multiply 15 by 12. The length of this ramp would need to be 180" or 15 feet. If the rise was 15" and you wanted a slope of 1:20, the ramp would need to be 300" long or 25 feet.

A gently sloping ramp of concrete offers accessibility and adds to your home's aesthetic appeal.

Photo courtesy Access One, Inc./
Beyond Barriers/Dave Regal Construction.

©Robert Perron

Design your ramp for comfortable use. Add shelter in areas where extreme weather is a factor.

Ramp Design

Sketch out a ramp design to fit your yard and entrance. If you need help with this step, contact an occupational therapist, a home remodeler, an architect, a national association on aging and disabilities, or the National Council on Independent Living (see Resources, page 138). Your state Veteran's Association also may be helpful.

Comfortable use should drive the design of your ramp. To prevent fatigue, all ramps should be level from side to side. Thresholds between doorsills and landings should not be higher than ¼", and gutters and shelter should be considered where weather is a factor. In addition, every ramp design should include the following features:

Ramp width should be between 32 and 48". Smaller widths may provide support for someone who can walk with handrail assistance on both sides; larger widths work better for someone who requires an assistant to walk beside them. A width of 36" generally provides enough space for walker, cane, or crutch use, and 42 to 48" works for wheelchair use.

Handrails should always be included on a ramp and provide support for at least 250 pounds. Check with your building department on local codes.

Handrail height will vary depending upon who uses the ramp. Wheelchair users usually need rails from 31 to 34". Walkers usually are more comfortable with handrails set at 36".

Round handrails provide better support than other styles. Select a diameter that is no more than 1½". You should be able to grip the rail comfortably between your thumb and fingers. Wood is preferred over metal, especially where weather is a factor.

Guardrails or curbing should be added to prevent wheelchairs, walkers, and canes from slipping off the ramp. Set guardrails at knee height when seated. Install curbing along the ramp's surface.

Landings are always included at the top of a ramp to allow a wheelchair or walker user to open the door on a level surface. Top landings should provide enough room to maneuver a wheelchair and open the door. Depending on the door swing, the landing should be between 48 and 60" wide and approximately 60" deep. Make sure the top landing and the door threshold do not vary by more than ¼".

Intermediate landings serve two functions: they provide a resting spot, and they create a turn in

Photo courtesy Handi-Ramp.

Prefabricated ramps are available in permanent and portable styles. Access heights and weight limits vary with style and material.

©Robert Perron

Handrails should always be included on a ramp and should provide support for at least 250 pounds.

Finish a ramp with a nonslip surface that works well when wet.

long ramps. As a general rule, include a landing for every 30" change in rise. You may choose to include extra landings if a family member requires more frequent rests to manage the incline.

All intermediate landings should match the ramp's width and provide a level stopping place. The size of the landing will depend on your ramp's slope and the turn required. Steeper inclines require larger landing areas. In general, consider a length between 36 and 60". Ninety-degree turns require approximately 48 × 48" for turning space. In switchback designs, the landing width should be twice the width of the ramp sections.

A bottom landing may be necessary to provide a transition area from the ramp to ground level. In these situations, the landing should equal the ramp's width and be 48 to 72" long, depending on the ramp's user.

Footings and bolting may be required or recommended for ramps and landings, depending on climate and soil conditions in your area. Check with your local building authority.

Construction Materials

In addition to post and beam wood styles, ramps can be built from grass, steel, synthetic lumber, concrete, brick, and asphalt. Choose materials and features that enhance your home's exterior. Concrete, for example, can be tinted, molded into "brick pavers," and scored to look like flagstone. Brick can be built up into pillars that serve as planters.

Surface Finish

Finish your ramp with a nonslip surface that works well when wet. Make sure the ramp's surface remains level. Texturize or brush concrete to help wheelchairs and walkers grip the ramp. Brush wood with a nonslip paint or sprinkle sand onto polyurethane to provide traction. Add grit tape to the ramp's surface.

Portable Ramps

If you need a ramp only occasionally or you will require one for only a short amount of time, a portable ramp may be the answer.

Portable ramps of aluminum or fiberglass can be transported to various locations and are constructed to accommodate scooters, wheelchairs, and van access. Access heights and weight limits vary with style and material.

A variety of models are available, including solid-surface, single-fold, track, suitcase, modular, roll-up, and multi-fold ramps. You can also find ready-made threshold and curb access ramps.

Electric Lifts

Vertical wheelchair lifts provide a compact alternative to ramp systems. While more expensive than ramps, electric lifts are a good choice when yard space is at a premium or disabilities prevent incline use.

Models are available for both exterior and interior installations, with various platform sizes, features, and options. Freestanding, hoistway, or concealed lifts provide comfort and security in exterior applications.

Lifts can be installed next to stairways, adjacent to deck platforms, and in garages, when space permits. See Resources, page 136, for information on vertical wheelchair lift manufacturers.

Concrete can be tinted, scored to look like flagstone, or molded into "brick pavers."

Photo courtesy Handi-Ramp.

Portable ramps come in a variety of styles to accommodate scooters, wheelchairs, and van access.

HOME IMPROVEMENT FUNDING

Many of the suggestions in this book are low-cost, do-it-yourself options for making your home more accessible. When your home requires extensive remodeling to make it accessible, look into home improvement financing for your project.

In an effort to help people with special needs stay in their homes, many federal, state, and local agencies have set aside public monies for accessible home modification. In addition, many corporate, private, and charitable organizations provide volunteer services or project donations to qualifying homeowners who need assistance. To find out if you qualify for these programs, contact your local or state housing department and ask about home modification funding assistance.

If you are remodeling a home for an elderly relative, check with local and national associations for information about special programs for seniors. These programs often provide referrals or contractors to perform no- or low-cost modification services for eligible elderly adults.

Ask every department and individual with whom you speak for a referral to an additional funding source. Funding often is available from a variety of departments. You'll also find additional resources at the end of this chapter.

Local Funding Sources

Possible local funding sources include state or county finance, public welfare, energy, and community development departments. Contact the National Council on Independent Living (NCIL) to find out if your state has an independent living council, an organization that provides local home modification funding and referrals.

Depending on your situation, other home modification funding sources may include your state vocational rehabilitation department, and the Veteran's Administration. Pending worker's compensation settlements may include home modifications.

Your local city, county, and state representatives can all provide information about home improvement funding and ramp installation. These community leaders can also tell you if you qualify for city or state property tax credits or abatements as a result of your home modifications. For information about federal tax deductions, contact the Internal Revenue Service (IRS) or your local tax accountant.

Don't overlook volunteer organizations. Many religious and community groups provide service work. One group is Christmas in April (also known as Rebuilding Together).

Ask your health care provider for information on Medicare and Medicaid funding. Medical equipment or home modifications may be covered by insurance when prescribed by a doctor. Be persistent—claims for equipment or modifications may require multiple applications.

Corporate Funding Sources

Corporate foundations make grants to support a variety of causes. Contact your library for a list of private foundations and how to qualify and apply for grants.

Societies & Associations

If your disability is the result of a progressive illness, you may be eligible for assistance from a national association. Depending upon your situation, consider contacting the American Cancer Society, the National Multiple Sclerosis Society, the National Muscular Dystrophy Association, or the National United Cerebral Palsy Association for assistance.

Federal Sources

The federal government has a variety of low-interest loan programs. The USDA Direct Rural Housing Loan Program and the USDA Guaranteed Rural Housing Loan Program offer loans to low- and moderate-income households.

The U.S. Department of Housing and Urban Development (HUD) has a variety of programs available for home modifications. Social Security funds may be available to you through the Plan for Achieving Self-Support (PASS) or Supplemental Security Income (SSI), which allows individuals to set up a dedicated savings plan without jeopardizing benefits.

If you are an elderly adult, contact the Local Area Agency on Aging to ask whether your home modification plans qualify for funds from the Older Americans Act Title III of the Administration on Aging.

Private Funding Sources

You may want to look into a personal or mortgage loan to supplement your home modification funds. The Access Home Modification Program is one program that offers loans to homeowners with disabled family members. Contact your local financial institution to learn about others.

How to Apply

You may be asked to fill out a form or submit a plan detailing the reason for the home modification, proposed projects, estimate of total cost, and amount of funding you seek. Many funding programs are set up on an income scale, and lower-income homeowners generally are eligible for more assistance.

Purchasing an Accessible Home

If you want to purchase a home that is designed to be accessible, contact the Accessible Customized Environments Program (ACE), which purchases, modifies, and makes accessible homes available to families with disabled members.

National Council on Independent Living
1916 Wilson Boulevard, Suite 209
Arlington, VA 22201
Telephone: (703) 525-3406
TTY: (703) 525-4153
Fax: (703) 525-3409
Web Site: www.ncil.org

Social Security Administration
Locate your local office in the Government Pages
of your phone directory.
Telephone: (800) 772-1213.
Web Site: www.ssa.gov

USDA Rural Housing Service
National Office
U.S. Department of Agriculture
Room 5037, South Building
14th Street and Independence Avenue, SW
Washington, DC 20250
Telephone: (202) 720-4323
Web Site: www.rurdev.usda.gov

**U.S. Department of Housing and
Urban Development (HUD)**
451 7th Street, SW
Washington, DC 20410
Telephone: (202) 708-1112
TTY: (202) 708-1455
Web Site: www.hud.gov

U.S. Department of Veterans Affairs (DVA)
Locate your local office in the Government Pages
of your phone directory.

National Office
810 Vermont Avenue, NW
Washington, DC 20420
Web Site: www.va.gov

**Accessible Customized Environments
Program (ACE)**
Extended Home Services
5230 Capitol Drive
Wheeling, IL 60096
Telephone: (847) 215-9490
Fax: (847) 215-9632
Web Site: www.ehls.com

**Christmas in April USA
(aka Rebuilding Together)**
1536 16th Street, NW
Washington, DC 20036-1402
Telephone: (202) 483-9083; 1-800-4-REHAB9
Fax: (202) 483-9081
Web Site: www.rebuildingtogether.org

Internal Revenue Service (IRS)
Locate your local office in the Government Pages of
your phone directory.
Web Site: www.irs.gov

American Cancer Society (ACS)
Locate your locate chapter in your phone
directory, or call (800) ACS-2345

National Multiple Sclerosis Society
733 Third Avenue
New York, NY 10017
Telephone: (800) Fight MS (1-800-344-4867)
Web Site: www.nationalmssociety.org

Muscular Dystrophy Association - USA
National Headquarters
3300 E. Sunrise Drive
Tucson, AZ 85718
Telephone: (800) 572-1717
Web Site: www.mdausa.org

National United Cerebral Palsy Association
1660 L Street, NW, Suite 700
Washington, DC 20036
Telephone: (800) 872-5827 or (202) 776-0406
TTY: (202) 973-7197
Fax: (202) 776-0414
Web Site: www.ucp.org

U.S. Department of Energy
1000 Independence Avenue, SW
Washington, DC 20585
Telephone: (800) DIAL-DOE
Fax: (202) 586-4403
Web Site: www.energy.gov

**National Association of Area Agencies
on Aging**
927 15th Street, NW, 6th Floor
Washington, DC 20005
Telephone: (202) 296-8130
Fax: (202) 296-8134
Web Site: www.n4a.org

FINDING CONTRACTORS

Homeowners often hire professional tradespeople to complete complex or specialized projects such as accessibility remodeling. But before the first nail is driven, consider consulting an occupational therapist, architect, designer, or builder to help you tailor the project to your specific needs.

Schedule a home visit from an occupational therapist to help identify safety issues for your family. These professionals understand the special needs of family members with age-related limitations or physical disabilities, and their insight can help you plan for the future, as well as for today.

If your home plans involve extensive remodeling, adding on, or retrofitting an existing home with special features, consult an architect who specializes in accessible design. For less-extensive modifications, a designer or a builder should suit your needs. Specialized designers are available to target specific rooms of your home, such as kitchens and baths. These specialists can help arrange for contractors to complete your project.

If you plan to complete some or all of the remodeling work yourself, or if you will act as general contractor for the project, contact your local building department early in the process. Find out which building codes apply to your project, which permits you must obtain, and which parts of the project must be completed by a licensed professional. At this meeting, you will also find out what plans and drawings you need to proceed with your project.

Sources

The best way to find a qualified tradesperson is to ask friends and relatives for referrals. Contact local and national support or advocacy groups for your disability and ask about contractors with accessible design experience in your area. You also can contact kitchen and bath design centers, design/build firms, builders' associations, local trade guilds, or lumberyards and home centers for lists of reputable contractors.

The Yellow Pages, home shows, and the Internet are other sources. Always check references—including a project currently underway, if possible.

In general, any contractor you consider should be located close to your home, have at least 5 years' experience with accessible design, and have a license and insurance, as well as endorsements or certifications.

Make phone calls to narrow your search. Tell prospective contractors you are making accessibility modifications, and ask if they are interested in the project.

Schedule home visits with good candidates. This gives you the opportunity to discuss estimates or price quotes, license numbers and insurance, and suppliers and references. It also

Hire a contractor located close to your home. He or she should have at least 5 years of experience in accessible design and a current license and insurance policy, as well as endorsements or certifications.

lets you evaluate the contractor's demeanor and work style.

Ask when the job can begin, how many people will be on the job, and who will take care of permits. This is also the time to discuss any work you plan to complete yourself.

Contracts

When you hire an architect, general contractor, or subcontractor to handle all or part of your project, you can delegate permit acquisition, planning, and construction drawings to them via your contract.

After you've selected a contractor, arrange a meeting to finalize arrangements and sign a contract. A good contract protects both you and the contractor. It spells out the work to be done, the payments to be made, and the responsibilities of each party.

A contract should be written to include any pertinent details, and it should include the following information:

- Description of the work at the specified address, including any work that you will complete.

- Itemization of the building permits required and who is responsible for obtaining them.

- Start and completion dates, as well as acceptable reasons for delay.

Schedule home visits with several contractors before you hire someone.

- Final inspection and "make good" arrangements.

- Total cost of the project.

- Amount and due date of each payment (usually ⅓ to ½ of the total cost as a down payment, with another payment at the project midpoint, and the last 15% or more paid after the work passes your final inspection).

- Change-order clause, specifying provisions and charges for changes made during the project (a markup of 10 to 15% is considered reasonable).

- Cleanup, indicating who is responsible for refuse collection and removal.

Remodeling projects create debris and temporary disarray that can be hazardous for people with disabilities. Ask your contractor if you should make alternate housing arrangements during the construction phase of your project.

CONTRACTORS & INFORMATION

These national organizations can provide you with information about home remodeling and accessibility projects for aging and disabled individuals. They can also help you locate qualified professionals in your area.

The American Occupational Therapy Association (AOTA)
4720 Montgomery Lane
P.O. Box 31220
Bethesda, MD 20824-1220
Telephone: (800) 668-8255 or
(301) 652-2682
TDD: (800) 377-8555
Fax: (301) 652-7711
Web Site: www.aota.org

National Association of Home Builders (NAHB)
1201 15th Street, NW
Washington, DC 20005
Telephone: (800) 368-5242 or
(202) 266-8200
Web Site: www.nahb.com

National Kitchen & Bath Association (NKBA)
687 Willow Grove Street
Hackettstown, NJ 07840
Telephone: (877) NKBA-PRO
Fax: (908) 852-1695
Web Site: www.nkba.org

RESOURCES

ABLEDATA
Telephone: (800) 227-0216
Fax: (301) 608-8958
Web Site: www.abledata.com
Information on assistive technology and
rehabilitation equipment.

Access One, Inc.
Telephone: (800) 561-2223
Web Site: www.beyondbarriers.com
Products that enhance freedom and
independence for disabled individuals.

Accessible Designs—Adjustable Systems, Inc.
94 North Columbus Road
Athens, OH 45701
Telephone: (614) 593-5240
Home environment products designed for
wheelchair access.

Adaptive Environments Center, Inc.
374 Congress Street
Suite 301
Boston, MA 02210
Telephone: (617) 695-1225 (V/TTY)
Fax: (617) 482-8099
Web Site: www.adaptiveenvironments.org
Information, technical assistance, and education
source on accessibility.

Alzheimer's Association
919 North Michigan Avenue
Suite 1100
Chicago, IL 60611-1676
Telephone: (800) 272-3900 or (312) 335-8700
Fax: (312) 335-1110
Web Site: www.alz.org
Information and support for individuals and fami-
lies confronted with Alzheimer's disease.

American Association of Retired Persons (AARP)
601 E Street, NW
Washington, DC 20049
Telephone: (800) 424-3410
Web Site: www.aarp.org
Education, lifestyle, health, news, and product
information for people over 50.

American Occupational Therapy Association, Inc.
4720 Montgomery Lane
P.O. Box 31220
Bethesda, MD 20824
Telephone: (301) 652-2682
Web Site: www.aota.org
Occupational therapy information, therapist refer-
rals, and product information for people requiring
occupational therapy.

Appliances for the Physically Challenged
Web Site: www.appliance411.com
Information about home appliances and installation options that enhance accessibility, as well as
links to other sites.

Association for Safe and Accessible Products
1511 K Street, NW, Suite 600
Washington, DC 20005
Telephone: (202) 347-8200
Information on and resources for safe and
accessible products.

Center for Inclusive Design
& Environmental Access (IDEA)
School of Architecture and Planning
University of Buffalo
Telephone: (716) 829-3485 ext. 329
Fax: (716) 829-3861
Web Site: www.ap.buffalo.edu/idea/
A University of Buffalo research center on universal
design and technical expertise in architecture,
product design, facilities management, and social
and behavioral issues.

Center for Universal Design
NC State University
School of Design
Campus Box 8613
Raleigh, NC 27695-8613
Telephone/TTY: (919) 515-3082
Fax: (919) 515-3023
InfoLine: (800) 647-6777
A national research, information, and technical assistance center that evaluates, develops, and promotes universal design in housing, public and commercial facilities, and related products.

Disabled American Veterans
National Service Headquarters
807 Mains Avenue, SW
Washington, DC 20024
Telephone: (202) 986-0375
Web Site: www.dav.org
A national organization developed to provide resources and information to American veterans of war.

Eastern Paralyzed Veterans Association
75-20 Astoria Boulevard
Jackson Heights, NY 11370
Telephone: (718) 803-EPVA
Fax: (718) 803-0414
Web Site: www.epva.org
Sample house plans, barrier-free design information, and links to resources.

Guldmann, Inc. America
5505 Johns Road, Suite 700
Tampa, FL 33634
Telephone: (800) 664-8834 or (813) 880-0619
Fax: (813) 880-9558
Web Site: www.stepless.com
Ramps, hoists, rail systems, and beds.

Home Automation Association
1444 I Street, NW, Suite 700
Washington, DC 20005
Telephone: (202) 712-9050
Fax: (202) 216-9646
Web Site: www.homeautomation.org
A trade association of manufacturers, distributors, dealers, installers and service providers of lighting, entertainment, security, telecommunications, heating and air conditioning systems that can be linked and automated.

Independent Living Research
Utilization Project
2323 S. Shepard Street, Suite 1000
Houston, TX 77019
Telephone: (713) 520-0232
TDD: (713) 520-5136
Fax: (713) 520-5785
Web Site: www.ilru.org
Information, training, research, and technical assistance in independent living.

Job Accommodation Network
P.O. Box 6080
Morgantown, WV 26506-6080
Telephone: (800) 526-7234 (V/TTY)
Fax: (304) 293-5407
Web Site: www.jan.wvu.edu
A free service of the Office of Disability Employment Policy of the U.S. Department of Labor that provides information about job accommodations, the Americans with Disabilities Act (ADA), and the employability of people with disabilities.

Lifease
2451 15th Street NW, Suite D
New Brighton, MN 55112
Telephone: (612) 636-6869
Web Site: www.lifease.com
A program developed to help people live independently and comfortably in their own homes as long as possible by linking them to products and ideas that can help.

National Association of Home Builders (NAHB)
Research Center
Telephone: (800) 638-8556
Fax: (301) 430-6180
Web Site: www.nahbrc.org
A research center with programs focused on issues such as senior housing and innovative ideas that incorporate new manufacturing and building materials and techniques.

National Association of the Remodeling Industry (NARI)
780 Lee Street, Suite 200
Des Plaines, IL 60016
Telephone: (847) 298-9200
Fax: (847) 298-9225
Web Site: www.nari.org
An association of contractors, design and building firms, manufacturers, suppliers, distributors, subcontractors, lenders, and others who work in the remodeling field that provides information and resources to homeowners considering remodeling.

National Center for Disability Services
201 I.U. Willets Road
Albertson, NY 11507
Telephone: (516) 747-5400
Web Site: www.ncds.org
A non-profit agency dedicated to helping people with disabilities live active, independent, and self-sufficient lives. Provides education, training, research, leadership, and example, and works to influence national attitudes, policies,and legislation.

National Council on Independent Living
1916 Wilson Boulevard, Suite 209
Arlington, VA 22201
Telephone: (703) 525-3406
TTY: (703) 525-4153
Fax: (703) 525-3409
Web Site: www.ncil.org
Advocacy, conferences, training, technical assistance, and information to help people with disabilities live with dignity and support in their homes and communities.

National Resource Center for Supportive Housing and Home Modifications
University of Southern California
Ethel Percy Andrus Gerontology Center
3715 McClintock Avenue
Los Angeles, CA 90089-0191
Telephone: (213) 740-6060
Fax: (213) 740-8241
Web Site: www.homemods.org
A source for information on architects, funding, modifications, universal design, products, manufacturers, and assistive technology.

National Rehabilitation Information Center (NRIC)
4200 Forbes Boulevard, Suite 202
Lanham, MD 20706
Telephone: (800) 346-2742 or (301) 459-5900
Web Site: www.naric.com
Disability information, research, products, and information.

Silver Cross
434 120th Street West, Suite 10E
New York, NY
Web Site: www.silvercross.com
Site for new, recycled, and low-cost lifts, scooters, elevators, and other equipment.

United States Administration on Aging
330 Independence Avenue, SW
Washington, DC 20201
Telephone Numbers:
(800) 677-1116 (Eldercare Locator)
(202) 619-7501 (technical information and public inquiries)
TTY: (800) 877-8339
Fax: (202) 260-1012
Web Site: www.aoa.dhhs.gov
Information and resources on aging.

United States Department of Housing and Urban Development (HUD)
451 7th Street SW
Washington, DC 20410
Telephone: (202) 708-1112
TTY: (202) 708-1455
Fax: (301)-519-5767
Web Site: www.hud.gov
Information and resources on home buying, home improvement, and funding.

Manufacturers

Access One, Inc.
5679 Gram Ford Ave.
Wyoming, MN 55092
Phone: (651) 462-3444
www.beyondbarriers.com

Anderson Windows, Inc.
Phone: (800) 426-4261
www.andersonwindows.com

Basketville
Main Street
Putney, VT 05346
Phone: (800) 258-4553
www.basketville.com

Bruno Independent Living Aids, Inc.
1780 Executive Drive, P.O. Box 84
Oconomowoc, WI 53066
Phone: (800) 882-883
www.bruno.com

California Closets
Phone: (800) 2SIMPLIFY
www.calclosets.com

CertainTeed EverNew
Phone: (800) 233-8990
www.certainteed.com

Closetworks
1001 W. North Ave.
Chicago, IL 60622
Phone: (312) 787-2290
www.closetworks.com

Dura Supreme, Inc.
300 Dura Drive
Howard Lake, MN 55349
Phone: (888) 711-3872
www.durasupreme.com

Economic Mobility, Inc.
6785 Forest Oak Drive
Clemmons, NC 27012
Phone: (800) 342-8801
www.toiletlift.com

Electrolux Home Products
250 Bobby Jones
Augusta, GA 30907
Phone: (800) FRIGIDAIRE
www.frigidaire.com

Elkay
2222 Camden Court
Oak Brook, IL 60523
Phone: (630) 574-8484
www.elkay.com

General Electric
Phone: (800) 626-2000
www.geappliances.com

The Genie Company
22790 Lake Park Boulevard
Alliance, OH 44601

Phone: (330) 821-5360
www.geniecompany.com

Ginger
460 N. Greenway Industrial Drive
Fort Mill, SC 29708
Phone: (888) 469-6511
www.gingerco.com

Handi-Ramp, Inc.
510 North Avenue
Libertyville, IL 60048
Phone: (800) 876-RAMP
www.handiramp.com

IKEA Home Furnishings
Phone: (800) 434-IKEA
www.IKEA.com

Intermatic, Inc.
Intermatic Plaza
Spring Grove, IL 60081
Phone: (815) 675-2321
www.intermatic.com

Kohler Co.
Phone: (800) 4-KOHLER
www.kohlerco.com

L.E. Johnson Products
2100 Sterling Ave.
Elkhart, IN 46516
Phone: (574) 293-5664
www.johnsonhardware.com

Levenger
420 South Congress Ave.
Delray Beach, FL 33445-4696
Phone: (800) 544-0880
www.levenger.com

Leviton
5925 Little Neck Parkway
Little Neck, NY 11362
Phone: (718) 281-6552
www.leviton.com

Lillian Vernon Catalog
Phone: (800) LILLIAN
www.lillianvernon.com

Nora Lighting
6505 Gayhart Street
Commerce, CA 90040
Phone: (800) 686-6672
www.noralighting.com

Room & Board
4600 Olson Memorial Highway
Minneapolis, MN 55422
Phone: (800) 486-6554
www.roomandboard.com

Simpson Door Co.
400 Simpson Ave.
McCleary, WA 98557
Phone: (800) 952-4057
www.simpsondoor.com

Smarthome, Inc.
16542 Millikan

Irvine, CA 92606
Phone: (800) SMARTHOME
www.smarthome.com

The Swan Corporation
One City Centre
St. Louis, MO 63101
Phone: (800) 325-7008
www.swanstone.com

Toggler Anchor System
Div. of Mechanical Plastics Corp.
P.O. Box 554
Elmsford, NY 10523-0554
Phone: (914) 347-2727
www.toggler.com

TOTO USA
1155 Southern Road
Morrow, GA 30260
Phone: (800) 350-8686
www.totousa.com

U-Line Corporation
Phone: (414) 354-0300
www.u-line.com

Weiser Lock
6700 Weiser Lock Drive
Tucson, AZ 85746
Phone: (800) 677-LOCK
www.weiserlock.com

Wellborn Cabinet, Inc.
38669 Highway 77 South
Ashland, AL 36251
Phone: (800) 336-8040
www.wellborn.com

Whirlpool
200 M 63 North
Benton Harbor, MI 49022
Phone: (800) 293-1301
www.whirlpool.com

WingIt Innovations, LLC
Phone: (877) 8WINGIT
www.wingits.com

Photographers

David Livingston
www.davidlivingston.com
©David Livingston: 42, 43.

Karen Melvin, Architectural Stock
Images, Inc.
Minneapolis, MN
©Karen Melvin: 92

Robert Perron
Branford, CT
©Robert Perron: 3, 8, 10, 64, 82, 83,
125, 126.

George Robinson
Grand Isle, VT
©George Robinson: 112, 116.

INDEX

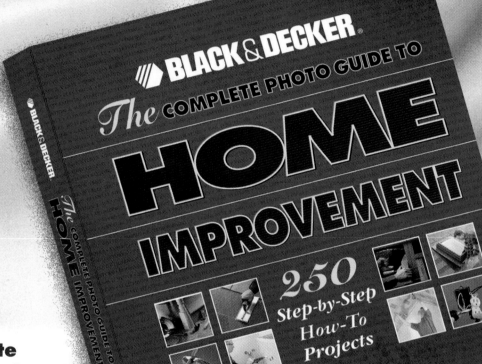

Also from

CREATIVE PUBLISHING INTERNATIONAL

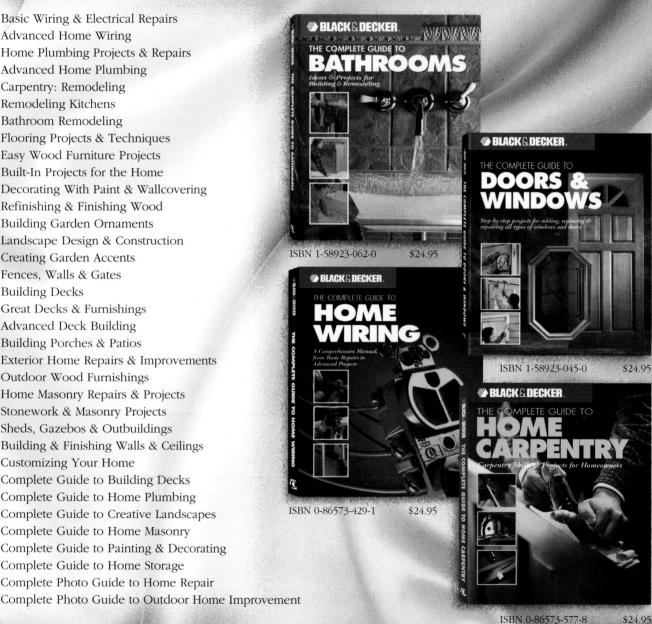

ISBN 1-58923-062-0 $24.95

ISBN 1-58923-045-0 $24.95

ISBN 0-86573-429-1 $24.95

ISBN 0-86573-577-8 $24.95

CREATIVE PUBLISHING INTERNATIONAL

18705 LAKE DRIVE EAST
CHANHASSEN, MN 55317

WWW.CREATIVEPUB.COM

TM80372-D
98